How to Leave Your Job and Buy a Business of Your Own

How to Leave Your Job and Buy a Business of Your Own

C. D. Peterson

McGraw-Hill Book Company

New York   St. Louis   San Francisco   Auckland
Bogotá   Hamburg   London   Madrid   Mexico
Milan   Montreal   New Delhi   Panama
Paris   São Paulo   Singapore
Sydney   Tokyo   Toronto

Library of Congress Cataloging-in-Publication Data

Peterson, C. D. (Carl D.)
  How to leave your job and buy a business of your own.

  Bibliography: p.
  Includes index.
  1. Business enterprises—Purchasing. I. Title.
HD1393.25.P48 1988   658.1'6   88-2948
ISBN 0-07-049633-1

ISBN 0-07-049633-1

1234567890   DOC/DOC   8921098

*The editors for this book were Martha Jewett and Nancy Young, the designer
was Naomi Auerbach, and the production supervisor was Dianne L. Walber. It
was composed by the McGraw-Hill Book Company Professional & Reference
Division Composition Unit.*

Printed and bound by R.R. Donnelley & Sons Company.

To Odessa, Wendy, Stephanie, and Chris

Contents

Preface

If you are bored in a dead-end job, if you face corporate cutbacks or retirement, or if you just have an unrelenting desire to change your lifestyle and be independent, this book can help you buy or start a business of your own. If you are a business broker, a financial advisor, or are involved in outplacement or career counseling, *How to Leave Your Job and Buy a Business of Your Own* can help you guide those who are considering this increasingly important course of action.

It is not a get-rich-quick book. It does not offer schemes to buy or start businesses with "no money down." It does not offer vignettes about T. Boone Pickens, Lee Iacocca, or the latest fast food franchise king.

It is a step-by-step guide that will show:

- What to do while you're still employed
- How to decide what you want
- How to determine what you can afford
- How to find the business
- How to buy the business

In addition, there are a number of appendixes. They include:

- Sources of information
- Conventional financing sources
- Sources of mailing lists
- Entrepreneurial support groups

- Industry guides
- Statistical sources
- Venture capital sources
- Government agencies
- Titles of useful books and magazines
- Sources of businesses available for sale

How to Leave Your Job and Buy a Business of Your Own can help you reduce the risk you will face by showing you how to gather and evaluate information which will prepare you to make better decisions. It will also show you how to keep from risking an investment too early in the process. And it includes two special chapters to help you examine franchises and the alternative of starting a business.

Finally, *How to Leave Your Job and Buy a Business of Your Own* provides worksheets for every step. These worksheets will help you convert your ideas into an organized program of action to get you on your way.

C.D. Peterson

Acknowledgments

I've chosen to acknowledge the enormous help I received in chronological order. Each person deserves all my thanks because, at the time each helped me, I truly needed it.

From the beginning, my family gave me 100 percent support and, more importantly, 100 percent faith.

Elizabeth Lawrence provided her always professional word processing and some valuable perspective.

My associates in my brokerage firm reviewed the roughest of drafts and helped make order out of chaos. They are Bill Couch, Barry Emmert, Art Freitas, Todd Kolb, Maureen Sperrazza, and Mary Ellen Giles. A special thanks to Duncan Haile for technical input.

My students in my small first class bore much the same burden and paid to do it. My thanks to Carol and John Comiskey, Claude Jack, Aaron Klapow, and Frank Kneece.

The accounting firm of Greenhaus, Bliss, Riordan & Co. gave much of their time to review and organize the financial content, and Marc Erdrich provided the facts on computer systems.

At the end, Martha Jewett, Jim Bessent, and Nancy Young at McGraw-Hill went the extra distance to bring this book out earlier rather than later.

1
Understanding the Background

Leaving a job to own a business is not a new idea, but it is a course of action that people are taking for some new reasons. Today, the long-standing American dream of independence is even more popular because of changes in corporate America and new encouragement for entrepreneurship. Added to this is the explosive growth of franchising, which opens up business ownership to those who are not necessarily wealthy or experienced.

Changes in Corporate America

For most of modern industrial history, a long-service corporate employee, particularly a manager, could be assured of continued employment if his or her performance was satisfactory. That's no longer true.

Corporate Cutbacks

Companies of all sizes are cutting back, laying off, and firing talented, productive people. The facts are well known:

- Mergers of large companies result in duplicate staffs. Whether on the basis of performance or politics, cuts are made and productive people are let go.

- Foreign competition has caused many firms to either shift production overseas or severely cut costs on domestic operations. Either way, good performers are left without jobs.

- Technology has caused whole industries, such as steel, to be restructured.

- Cost-reduction programs now focus on eliminating jobs as a way to lower costs.

Even IBM and AT&T, always considered "lifetime employers," have cut back tens of thousands of people. *Business Week,* in its October 5, 1987, issue provides some historical background. Beginning in the 1960s, a new phenomenon developed: The balance of payments shifted, making the United States a net importer. Overseas competitors, who were now finished rebuilding their businesses after World War II, became very aggressive.

When the exchange rates were allowed to float in 1971, the dollar fell. While this made U.S. goods more competitive to sell, it made the now much larger flow of imports more expensive to buy. Then came the oil crisis and inflation was racing at a full gallop. Inflation hit corporate profits, too, lulling some companies into expensive and self-perpetuating cost-of-living formulas for wage increases. Because cost increases could easily be passed through as price increases, improvements in efficiency and productivity were neglected.

> Companies became trapped in the worst of all possible worlds. By the late 1970s, even though profits still seemed strong, productivity growth was slowing to a crawl. The competitiveness of American manufacturers, as measured by their shares of world markets, was sagging. The Federal Reserve Board pushed up interest rates to fight inflation, and the dollar soared. American companies had to cope with higher credit costs while being priced out of markets overseas and surrendering big chunks of their domestic markets to cheaper and better imports.
>
> The adjustment has been painful. Plant closings, layoffs, restructuring, mergers, and acquisitions have provided the "leitmotiv" of the corporate drama for at least five years. Some industries have undergone wholesale elimination of excess capacity in a process of consolidation designed to carve up a shrinking pie among fewer companies.

The Baby Boomers

Another phenomenon is affecting job security. The huge bulge in our population that is known as the "baby boom," shown in Figure 1.1, is beginning to reach the narrower parts of the corporate ladder. Competition is keener and promotional progress is becoming slower and less sure. With this excess of human talent, the individual has less power and leverage.

Whether it is called early retirement, voluntary severance, or a layoff,

The age group in its mid-twenties to mid-thirties once was about equal in size to the group in its mid-forties to mid-fifties; it is now twice the size.

Population—U.S. Census (millions)		
	1960	1985
25 to 34	22	42
45 to 54	21	22

Figure 1.1. The impact of the baby boomers.

the result is the same—the previous, if unspoken, contract of continued employment in exchange for good work no longer exists. Hard work no longer equals job security. In a free economic system, these actions by companies are proper responses to markets and competition. The individual faced with unemployment also has proper economic responses. He or she can go seek out another job in another company or industry and hope that this employment experience will not suffer the same fate as the last one. Or the individual can follow a path that has become increasingly viable, owning a business.

Severance Programs

Corporations have made owning a business a more viable alternative by providing financial support. Severance payments and benefit coverage may run several months or even a year or more. Pension service is often adjusted to "bridge" the time required to qualify for benefits.

The corporate action which has contributed most to promoting entrepreneurship is the decline of job security as a reason to work for a company. If organizational employment can't provide job security, one of the major arguments in favor of working for someone else no longer exists.

Encouragement for Entrepreneurship

Wanting to eliminate the vagaries of working for others is not the only reason entrepreneurship is becoming more popular. Today it's easier to become an entrepreneur. In addition to corporate severance payments and benefits, there are three factors which encourage entrepreneurship: *franchises,* a *new infrastructure,* and the *American drive for independence.*

Franchises—Turnkey Entrepreneurship

Franchises offer some special appeals, particularly to the first-time business owner. Most come with tested systems to help manage the business. From the sign over the front door to the payroll accounting system, the franchisee has the franchisor's experience and support available. Many established franchisors have field consultants who visit the locations on a regular basis and who can be called to help with problems.

A common expression used to describe owning a franchise is "be in business for yourself but not by yourself." Owning a franchise can make the buyer instantly a part of a large organization with sophisticated advertising and strong market recognition.

Buying a franchise is a fairly straightforward proposition. Federal and state laws require the franchisor to disclose the material facts about the franchise and the offer to sell. There is little or no negotiating. This is considerably different from buying an established, nonfranchise business for which financial data may be vague and the price is determined only after lengthy negotiations.

The franchise industry enjoys a better reputation now than in years past, and it is growing rapidly, as shown in Fig. 1.2. The super successes in the field such as McDonald's, coupled with tight government regulation, have raised the image of franchises. While there are still bad franchises and dishonorable franchisors, there is generally a more positive view toward franchise ownership.

Franchises are now available in a wide variety and price range. One recent collection of franchise offerings contained a $3000 franchise to provide business education seminars and a $1 million top-name restaurant franchise. In between were franchises for instant printing

---

It is estimated that by the end of the century half the retail sales in the U.S. will be made through franchised outlets.

	1970	1987(est.)
Number of establishments	396,000	500,000
Dollar sales	$120 billion	$625 billion
Employment	2.5 million	6.3 million

Figure 1.2. The growth of franchising.

($35,000), hair styling ($75,000), automotive repair ($100,000), and even a basketball franchise for $250,000.

This variety means people have more chance to find opportunities which match their desires and their financial capabilities, making franchises attractive and affordable to more people who are seeking to become entrepreneurs.

An Infrastructure Now Exists to Support Entrepreneurship

Two new fixtures in American business, the personal computer and the business "networks," are good examples of the support infrastructure for entrepreneurs.

The Personal Computer. The personal computer allows individuals and smaller businesses to undertake projects, maintain controls, do analyses, and handle communications in ways formerly reserved for only larger firms. With a personal computer and a few accessories, a small business owner can have access to huge databases of information and to additional computing power.

Business Networks. The business networks may be an even more important element of the new entrepreneurial infrastructure. These networks include venture capital groups in which people with ideas and a need for capital regularly meet with those who have capital to invest. Lots of other entrepreneurial activity goes on at these meetings: consulting arrangements are made, acquisitions and mergers are pursued, partnerships are conceived, and so on.

Another very effective and relatively new network phenomenon is the "Tips Club." This is typically a group of 10 to 30 people who represent noncompeting businesses. Meetings are most often weekly early morning sessions over coffee, and they last about an hour. The club has only one purpose and that is to generate business for its members. Members are expected to patronize each other as much as is practical, but the real objective is for members to bring business leads and tips to each meeting. Members often ask for help with special leads and introductions. Some clubs have tough requirements for continued membership. Really effective clubs have a waiting list for membership. Forming a new club is a simple matter of getting a few business people together.

The Long-Standing American Admiration and Desire for Independence Still Lives

The spector of real or potential severance from employment is only one reason to consider a business of your own. Owning a business can mean independence, the opportunity to excel, a chance to do what you want, a way to build for you and your family, and the satisfaction of setting and meeting your own goals. It can also be the best investment you can make under the new tax laws. Of course, owning a business doesn't automatically mean wealth, happiness, and financial security.

Whether you see yourself standing among the plantings in your tree nursery, consulting with your staff in your electronics plant, winning a major client for your agency, or greeting guests in your restaurant, you know that technology and competition can affect any business. Owning a business can mean long hours and high financial risk. Stress can affect the entrepreneur as much as the employee.

The difference is one of personal control. Instead of the impotence often experienced as an employee, a business owner can take action and make choices and decisions. While the outcome may be no better, most competent productive people, if given a choice, would bet on themselves to do the best job of looking out for their own interests.

Concerns about health and stress, a desire to be more involved with family, and a strong need to set one's own personal standards of conduct and performance can all potentially be satisfied by owning a business.

Before proceeding, you should take a moment to ask yourself why you want your own business. You may have at least six other alternatives: a different job, a different company, consulting, teaching, government service, or even retirement. While reasons vary from security to wealth and while there are no right or wrong reasons, it is important to know why you want your own business. Owning a business had better satisfy these basic criteria or you will be no better off than you are now. Worksheet 1, which follows, will help you focus on these fundamental criteria.

Worksheet 1
Why Do You Want Your Own Business?

For each of the following statements, mark your degree of agreement; 0 equals no agreement at all and 5 equals complete agreement.

Statement of Reason	Degree of Agreement 0-5
I just can't stand to work for anyone anymore.	_____
I'm tired/bored doing what I'm doing.	_____
I want to get (very) rich.	_____
I feel insecure working for someone else.	_____
I want something I can really commit to.	_____
I have good reason to know that I can handle risk, especially personal risk.	_____
I don't like being around so many people.	_____
I want to work less (more).	_____
I want to travel less (more).	_____
I want to build something of my own.	_____
I can afford to fail.	_____
I would like the feeling of owning my own business.	_____
I want to move somewhere else.	_____
I can do without status symbols.	_____
I have an idea/a concept I want to pursue.	_____
I want to do something that can really grow.	_____
I want to stand out.	_____
I feel like a servant.	_____
I want to be properly rewarded for my efforts.	_____
I want to build something my family can get involved in.	_____
I don't like the politics and inefficiencies of corporate life.	_____
I want a lifestyle with more _____ and less _____.	_____
I have full family support in this effort.	_____
I don't like being so dependent on others.	_____
I've tried finding a job and can't find what I want.	_____
I'll never get promoted where I am.	_____
I'd gladly pinch pennies if I had to.	_____
I don't like all the organizational competition.	_____
I'm being held back working for someone else.	_____
Other: _____	

The purpose of this worksheet is to help you articulate your feelings and to start you thinking about the benefits and drawbacks of having your own business. Scoring your answers is simply a way to see which of them is important to you. When you are done, complete these sentences:

I want my own business because _____

_____

I think I can be successful in my own business because _____

_____

There are two ways the worksheet can be used:
1. Use this analysis to think through whether owning a business will satisfy the reasons you gave for considering it. For example, if you don't like being dependent on others, owning your own business is no guarantee you'll be free of dependency. You may become very dependent on customers or key employees. Owning a business entails much risk. You may want to consider just changing jobs.
2. Save this analysis to check against specific companies you will uncover later. After all your search and work, if the company can't satisfy these basic emotional criteria, you might want to reconsider.

2
Preparing While You're Still Employed

No matter what your reason—boredom, a dead-end job, corporate cutbacks, or just an unrelenting desire to be on your own—you can do a lot about owning your own business while you still have a job. You don't have to give up your salary and benefits because you don't have to give up working. Much of the preliminary work can be done in your off-hours and spare time.

There are examples of people getting their own businesses completely acquired and up and running while still keeping their jobs. Others have put major steps of the process in place before they resigned or before the severance clock started ticking. In his book, *Mail Order Moonlighting* (Ten Speed Press, Berkley, Calif., 1976), Cecil C. Hoge, Sr., offers a whole plan on how to start a mail-order business at home while keeping your job.

At the least, your analysis and fact finding can be done with less than full-time effort. Most of the time you will be making inquiries and waiting for responses. A good bit of your time should be spent reflecting on your motivation and commitment and on determining the kind of business you want. You do not have to jump off an economic cliff just yet.

Maximizing Your Severance Benefits

The first step, for those employed, is to fully understand and to lock in all the compensation and benefits your company policies and practices

9

provide. Companies will sometimes bend these policies and the practices can vary with circumstances.

Terms of severance, early retirement, and even resignation can be subject to some degree of negotiation. Negotiating a resignation may sound odd, but it is done. Whether out of conscience, fairness, guilt, or fear, employers will, on occasion, extend some form of severance benefits to a person who is resigning.

An example of negotiated separation occurs when a company is planning a large-scale cutback. The cutback may be done all at once, or it may be spread over a long period. To minimize the impact on its people, the company may ask employees to volunteer to be separated. While a general severance "package" is offered, companies typically offer variations to try and satisfy individual employees' needs. Older employees, minority employees, and those in other protected classes receive the attention normally accorded them. While the company is trying to ease the burden for its people, it is also, understandably, trying to limit its exposure to employee suits for discrimination or unlawful discharge. The Human Resources or Personnel Department is typically the keeper of the general policies. In some companies, this department controls all policy exceptions. In others, department heads or other executives can influence severance policies.

Depending on your company and your personal situation and relationships, you may go directly to the Human Resources Department or to a senior executive with whom you have a good relationship. If you know and can trust the discretion of anyone who has recently been subject to termination or severance, you might inquire about their experience to get a good fix on actual practices.

Some Considerations:

- What is the length of the salary continuation period? Are exceptions being made? Can other elements of the package be traded for more time? A very easy way to lengthen the period is to negotiate a later date to start it. In some cases, employees can negotiate a lump sum (though lower) payment.

- Which benefits and insurances are continued and for how long? Some benefits, such as employee discounts, are relatively low cost and might be easy to have extended. Most insurance coverages run coincidental with employment. Some states have now passed laws requiring that terminated employees be provided the opportunity to obtain insurance coverage. Seek this opportunity, but don't jump to buy it. The insurance offered may not be the same coverage your company had and it may be very high priced. The purpose of the legislation was to insure that people would not be left without any opportunity to buy some coverage. When negotiating for extended insurance coverage, be sensitive to how the insurance carrier calculates coverage periods. One day's service in a month or quarter may extend coverage for the full period.

■ How will your retirement credits be calculated and what is the status of your pension? This item is subject to detailed regulations. Obtain copies of your company's pension plan and have it explained. While the safety, administration, vesting, and payout schedules of your plan are narrowly prescribed, the calculation of length of service, credit for broken service, and so-called "bridging" or extending service in order to allow an employee to meet the threshold requirements of pension eligibility are subjects for negotiation.

■ What happens to deferred compensation, stocks, options, and savings plans your company is holding for you? While regulations do apply, practices vary, so check your firm's approach. Because your company may have recorded the liability of owing you these assets, they may be willing to ease the rules on how long they must be held. As with all of these compensation elements, you won't know if you don't ask.

■ What happens to accrued vacation and sick days? What are the provisions for earned but unpaid bonuses and commissions? These are things within a company's control and are implemented through well-known and accepted practices. Be sure you understand how to use the vacation and sick days best to lengthen your salary continuation and benefits coverage.

■ Are you entitled to relocation benefits? In some cases, employees who are transferred and then severed within a relatively short time or who are transferred under conditions considered to be temporary are entitled to be relocated in their "home" location.

■ Can you become a part-time consultant to your present company? Can you become an independent contractor or work on a special project? In addition to providing income, these arrangements might allow for benefits to be continued or for the time to be credited toward retirement. These arrangements allow companies to technically achieve their goals of reducing employees while allowing them to get important work done by qualified people.

■ Are you entitled to outplacement counseling? This fringe benefit can be very useful to you and very costly to your company. (Costs average 10 percent of your salary.) Most outplacement programs help individuals examine several alternatives for their future: retirement, a similar position in the same industry, a similar position in a different industry, a position in academia or with the government, a consulting practice, and the alternative of starting or buying a business. If you are entitled to outplacement help, ask that your program include this last alternative.

- Are you entitled to any support services? Quite often a company will provide secretarial and phone service and the use of an office for some period of time. Ask about services that can be used in your search for a company. This would include things like the company's library, the use of a computer, mailing privileges, use of financial reporting services such as Dun and Bradstreet, or even legal advice from the company's attorneys.

Guidelines

No matter which of the above elements you decide to pursue, there are three general guidelines to follow:

1. Understand the legal and personal tax implications of these compensation and benefit items. There may be large amounts of money involved. You need advice, so get professionals in the field. (More on professional advisors later in this chapter.)

2. Be pleasant and businesslike in your dealings with your company, even if you feel bitter. You will get more help that way. You can always get angry or sue later, and you never know when you might want to use the company or some of the people in the company as references.

3. If you don't ask what exceptions or additions to policies and practices you can have, you'll never know what extra help could have been yours. As you read on, you will see that some of this help can be very useful in your search for a company.

Worksheet 2 can help you itemize these benefits and establish negotiating objectives.

Selecting Your Advisors

Another step to take while you are still employed is to select your advisors. Here is a list of some key professionals you may need:

Accountant	Appraiser
Attorney	Banker
Business broker	Consultants
Financial planner	Insurance agent
Real estate broker	Stockbroker

You may already have a relationship with some of these advisors. Others you may not need for some time. Whenever you make your choices, you need to select these people on two criteria: competence and willingness.

Competence

Are they competent in their field as it relates to what you want to do: buy a business? Almost all of these professional fields have special areas of interest. The attorney who prepared your will may not be experienced in negotiating a purchase agreement for a business. Your real estate broker may have no contacts in the commercial or industrial field, and your banker may be involved in only consumer services. In most cases, your advisors will be candid and, if they are not qualified, will refer you to someone who is.

Willingness

Do they want to work with you in this effort? Not every qualified professional cares to work in this field. It's complicated, a high percentage of the transactions fall through, and the responsibility is significant. Be sure your advisors do want to work with you. Ideally, they should be enthusiastic and supportive while at the same time providing you with sound advice and protection.

After you have selected your advisors, record their names, addresses, and phone numbers (including home phone numbers) and have them handy at all times. It's normal to need advice in a hurry. Get them to know each other so that they become a team for you. Worksheet 3 will help you organize this information on your advisors.

Getting Ready Early

There are dozens of minor and not so minor steps involved in setting up to own your own business. Don't delay starting on them because they do take time to complete. These are "generic" steps and will be applicable to any business venture.

Form a Corporation

The largest percentage of business sales transactions are technically asset purchases, not the purchase of the stock of the corporation. The reasons why will be covered in Chapter 7, but the result is that you will probably need to form your own corporation to be able to purchase the assets. Under some conditions, you may want to establish yourself as a sole proprietor or form a partnership rather than a corporation. Table 2.1 compares the three forms of organization over a range of tax and expense considerations. Your attorney can show you how to provide for a corporate charter broad enough to conduct virtually any line of business. The process is simple, costs $1000 or less, and can be fun as you pick out a name and become a corporate officer in your own company.

Establishing the form of your business is important because it permits you to apply for the proper state and federal identification numbers which will be needed for other purposes.

Establish a Location

Eventually you will need a base of operations from which to conduct your search. There are lots of ways to establish a location, even if it is temporary. At the top of the cost ladder is renting and furnishing an office. Next is renting space in a cooperative office. Under this arrangement, you have a furnished office and share the reception and secretarial services with the other tenants. You might share an office with someone you know who has space for you. Another level of service is one that will receive your mail and phone calls but may or may not actually have office space for you to use. Of course, you can use your home as your location. You can augment your in-home location with a post office box, an answering service or answering machine, a separate phone line, and secretarial services purchased as necessary. At some point, you will probably consider a computer. Figure 2.1 explains some alternatives.

Order Business Cards and Stationery

Whether you use your new company name or just your own name, you need these essential business tools. Establishing credibility with sellers,

Table 2.1 Legal Forms of Organization

Consideration	Sole proprie-torship	Partnership		Corporation	
		General	Limited	C Corporation	S Corporation
Complexity of formation and opera-tion	Simple	Relatively sim-ple most of the time	More com-plex, requires written agreement and state filing	Most com-plex, requires state charter, election of officers, and directors, ₣ etc.	Same as a C corporation in legal op-eration and formation
Limits on number of owners or shareholders	1	Unlimited	Unlimited	Unlimited	Limited to 35 shareholders
Owners' per-sonal liability for business debts and claims of litigation	Unlimited personal liability	Unlimited personal liability	Generally lim-ited to amount of investment	Generally not liable for corporate debts, with a potential exception for Federal withholding taxes	Same as a C corporation
Federal in-come taxa-tion of busi-ness profits	Tax paid by owner at individual rates	Tax paid by partner at individual rates	Tax paid by partner at individual rates	Tax paid by corporation at corpora-tion rates	Tax paid by shareholders at individual rates
Deduction of business losses by owners	Yes, provided active partici-pation by owner	Yes, but lim-ited to amounts personally at risk and pas-sive loss rates	Yes, but lim-ited to amounts personally at risk and pas-sive loss rates	No	Yes, but lim-ited to in-vestment in stock and loans to the corporation; also subject to passive loss rates
Taxation of dividends or other with-drawals of profits	No	No	No	Yes	No

Table 2.1. Legal Forms of Organization (*Continued*)

Consideration	Sole proprie-torship	Partnership		Corporation	
		General	Limited	C Corporation	S Corporation
Social security tax on own-ers' earnings	13.02% up to $45,000 of earnings (with sched-uled annual increases)	Same as sole proprietor	No	15.02% of shareholder/ employee earnings up to $45,000 (with sched-uled annual increases); 50% paid by corporation, 50% paid by employee.	Same as C corporation for salaries
Unemploy-ment taxes	No	No	No	Yes, both fed-eral and state gener-ally	Yes, both fed-eral and state gener-ally
Availability of deductible qualified deferred compensa-tion plans for retire-ment	Yes, however borrowing prohibited	Yes, however borrowing prohibited	No	Yes, including the ability to borrow	Yes, however borrowing prohibited by 5% share-holder/ employee
Medical, dis-ability, and group term life insur-ance on owners	Generally not deductible; however, 25% of med-ical insur-ance is	Same as sole proprietor	Same as sole proprietor-ship	Corporation deduction generally not taxable to employee under cer-tain condi-tions.	Generally not deductible if paid for a 2% or more shareholder
Available op-tions of re-porting year	Limited to calendar year	Must conform to year end of majority partners	Same as gen-eral partner-ship	Any 12-month pe-riod, except for personal service cor-porations	Must conform to year end of majority shareholders (exception provided for natural busi-ness year)

Table 2.1. Legal Forms of Organization (*Continued*)

Consideration	Sole proprie-torship	Partnership		Corporation	
		General	Limited	C Corporation	S Corporation
Ability to allocate income among several owners	No	Yes	Yes	No	Yes
Automobile expenses	Deductible to extent of business use; maintain records	Same as sole proprietorship	No	Same as sole proprietorship	Same as C corporation
Business meals and entertaining	Deductible to the extent of 80% of ordinary and necessary expenses of carrying on a trade or business; maintain adequate records	Same as sole proprietorship	No	Same as sole proprietorship	Same as C corporation

financial sources, and others can be a critical factor and proper cards and stationery can help.

Open a Bank Account

You'll need a bank account for your company and the cost to set one up is low. As we mentioned earlier, be sure the bank you choose wants your type of account.

Apply for a Home Equity Credit Line

This flexible, low-cost line of credit can be a cornerstone of your financial strategy. The psychological hurdle of obtaining what is essentially a second mortgage on your home can be overcome if you consider that

Figure 2.1. Choosing a computer system.

The three components of a personal computer system are the computer, the printer, and the software programs.

The brand name of computer you buy makes very little difference, as long as you stick with advertised brands. The important considerations are:

- How easy is it to get service?

- Are all the parts (monitor, keyboard, printer, etc.) compatible?

- Will it run the programs that you need to operate your business?

- Is the system available with an internal hard disk drive?

- Will the dealer who sells you the computer provide assistance when you have a problem?

Software is another story. The programs you purchase make all the difference in how easy or difficult it will be to operate your business. Don't be tempted to buy every piece of software that comes along. Do some research first. Find out if you can get a demo disk before you buy. Don't buy any software until you look at the documentation. Don't be tempted to do your own programming unless you know that you will have at least as much time to become a computer expert as you will have to run your business. If you belong to a professional organization, find out what software they recommend. Before you buy any software, read the license agreement carefully. Remember, you are purchasing a license to *use* the product. It does not belong to you even after you purchase it. Find out how much upgrades cost and whether the vendor provides a toll-free number to answer your questions.

Here are some realistic estimates of the cost of a complete package:

System A (inexpensive). For basic accounting, in-house word processing, mailing lists, spreadsheets, etc. IBM XT or equivalent (Leading Edge Model D, Epson Equity I, PC-Clone, or basic Apple computer) with 88-key keyboard, monochrome (i.e., black and white, green, or amber) monitor, 20-megabyte hard disk drive, *non*letter-quality dot matrix printer, off-the-shelf software: $1800–$2400

System B (moderate). For double entry accounting, high-speed processing, graphics, letter-quality printing for advertising promotion, etc. IBM AT or equivalent, 101-key advanced keyboard, EGA color monitor, 20-megabyte hard drive, high-speed letter-quality printer, cut sheet feeder, customized and off-the-shelf software: $3300–$4500

System C (expensive). All the capability of System B plus the latest in microcomputer technology such as desktop publishing. Compaq 386 or equivalent (or IBM Model 80 or Apple II), laser printer, 40-megabyte disk drive, custom software plus off-the-shelf software as needed: $7700–$11,000

(Continued)

Figure 2.1. Choosing a computer system. (*Continued*)

> The above examples are a guide. Any of these configurations can be mixed and matched to give you precisely the system you want. Keep in mind that no matter what system you buy it will be outmoded in 24 to 36 months. It's a good idea to consider a computer as a recurring expense. Unless you have the available cash, you might want to think about a straight lease or an operating lease (which is equivalent to renting). Each method has its advantages and disadvantages.
>
> Add 10 to 15 percent annually to the above amounts for maintenance and supplies.

somewhere in this process of buying a business you will be asked to personally guarantee your borrowings. This type of loan can actually give you more control.

There are three important considerations with home equity loans:

- The interest rate, terms, and charges vary considerably from institution to institution, so shop carefully.

- Even though you may have substantial equity in your home, most lenders will still require evidence of your ability to repay the loan. You stand a better chance of being approved if you can substantiate a steady income.

- They take a long time to obtain. Because they are a form of mortgage, you will have to go through all the steps of application, including obtaining an appraisal. Further delays can be expected because recent changes in the tax laws favor this type of credit and many people are submitting applications, which lengthens the processing time.

Do Your Personal Preparation

If you believe you will need a special license or permit, get started now. Read books and attend seminars which you feel will help you. Talk with consultants and industry people. If you possibly can, talk with people who have done what you are planning to do. They can provide interesting if not entirely relevant insights. And keep track of all your expenses as you go through this process. Many of them are allowable business expenses. Figure 2.2 will give you some idea of the costs involved in setting up. Worksheet 4 can help you manage these necessary set-up steps that could cause critical delays later.

Deciding what else can be done while you are still employed will be a matter of your personal situation, your relationship with your company, and other factors. The important things are to be aware of how much can be done and to consciously manage this important time of transition.

The costs of getting set up for your business search are very modest:	
Forming a corporation	$500 to $750
State filing fees	$200 to $300
If complicated stockholder agreements are required or if you plan to form a partnership, add at least	$1000
500 high-quality business cards	$25
1000 sheets premium-grade imprinted letterhead and envelopes (first time; reorders are less)	$175 to $200
Office space and furnishings can vary. Check out the new executive office setups as a way to go. If you can satisfy your telephone and secretarial service, your home is your least costly office.	—
If you will need to replace your medical insurance, a basic nongroup family plan will cost approximately	$200 to $300/ month

Figure 2.2. The cost of setting up.

Worksheet 2
Locking in Your Compensation and Benefits

Compensation or Benefit Item	Company Policy or Practice*	Your Objective	Contact Person in the Company	Status
Salary continuation start date				
Length of salary continuation (dollars $ _____)				
Insurances:				
1. Health				
2. Life				
3. Dental				
4. _____				
5. _____				
Retirement:				
1. Length of service credits				
2. Bridging				
3. Payments				
4. Vesting				
5. _____				
Deferred compensation:				
1. Stock				
2. Savings				
3. _____				
4. _____				
5. _____				
Accrued compensation:				
1. Vacation				
2. Sick days				
3. Commissions/bonuses				
4. _____				
5. _____				
Relocation services				
Outplacement counseling				
Support services:				
1. Secretarial				
2. Office space				
3. Computer usage				
4. _____				
5. _____				
6. _____				
Part-time employment				

*If you are resigning or otherwise have the option of deciding when you will leave, check to make sure you are not leaving just short of some date which would qualify you for certain benefits.

Worksheet 3
Your Personal Advisors

Consider accountants, attorneys, appraisers, bankers, brokers, consultants, financial planners, insurance agents, stockbrokers, and anyone else you will be using to help you.

Competence relates to the advisor's experience and knowledge in the purchase/sale of businesses.

Willingness relates to the advisor's desire to work on your business-buying activities.

Name/ Profession	Address	Business Phone Home Phone	Competence	Willingness	Comments
_____	_____	_____	_____	_____	_____
_____	_____	_____			_____
	_____				_____
	_____				_____
_____	_____	_____	_____	_____	_____
_____	_____	_____			_____
	_____				_____
	_____				_____
_____	_____	_____	_____	_____	_____
_____	_____	_____			_____
	_____				_____
	_____				_____
_____	_____	_____	_____	_____	_____
_____	_____	_____			_____
	_____				_____
	_____				_____
_____	_____	_____	_____	_____	_____
_____	_____	_____			_____
	_____				_____
	_____				_____

Worksheet 4
Getting Set Up

Item	Estimated ($)	Action Planned	Date Next Step	Status
Establish a location	_____	_____	_____	_____
Business cards/stationery	_____	_____	_____	_____
Open a bank account	_____	_____	_____	_____
Apply for home equity line	_____	_____	_____	_____
Personal preparation				
· Reduce expenses	_____	_____	_____	_____
· Save	_____	_____	_____	_____
· Attend classes/read	_____	_____	_____	_____
· Obtain license	_____	_____	_____	_____
· Second job	_____	_____	_____	_____
· Spouse's job	_____	_____	_____	_____
· Join network:	_____	_____	_____	_____
_____	_____	_____	_____	_____
_____	_____	_____	_____	_____
_____	_____	_____	_____	_____
Form a corporation, partnership, or proprietorship	_____	_____	_____	_____

3
Deciding What You Want

Now that you've safeguarded what you already have (your benefits), it's time to really examine the idea of buying your own business, starting with the kind of business you might want. We will do this in two steps. Step 1 will establish your personal inventory of knowledge, skills, and traits. Step 2 will establish the business criteria, which includes how much money you need (and want), location, risk liquidity, growth, working conditions, status, people intensity, competition, and the actual content of the business.

Taking Your Personal Inventory

You want a business that you can enjoy owning and managing. But to be able to manage it at all, you need to have, or be willing to get, the essential knowledge and skills required to do so. We start by taking a personal inventory. The inventory is purposely divided into three parts: knowledge, skill, and traits. Use Worksheet 5; it is at the end of the chapter.

Knowledge

Things you know: Don't restrict this list to things from your work experience. Your family, sports, hobbies, vacations, or other interests all provide things you know. Ask yourself this question: "What five things do I know more about than almost anybody?" Rank them. While you're at it, go ahead and list five things you know the least about. Most of us find this an easy list to develop.

Skills

Things you can do: The same ground rules apply. The question this time is: "What five things can I do better than almost anybody? Do the reverse list of things you do poorly. It's not as easy an exercise as you might think, and it will be helpful later to clearly recognize your skills as well as your deficiencies.

Traits

Things you are: Complete this sentence five times, "I am...." Concentrate on your physical and mental attributes.

The Differences among Them

The separation of the above three categories has been done to emphasize the differences among them:

Knowledge can usually be acquired by study. If you want to see whether you have some particular knowledge, you can take a test or answer some questions. Skill, on the other hand, is a thing that you do. Skill comes from practice. While most people can reasonably expect to acquire knowledge by studying, there is no such expectation that a person can acquire skills by practicing. As an example, you can study and learn all there is to know about juggling, but you may never have the skill to do it well no matter how much you practice. You may improve with practice, but you could remain relatively unskilled. This distinction becomes important when we look at the essential requirements of a business. If you are deficient in knowledge (knowledge of the product line in a distribution business), you can probably overcome it. If you are deficient in a skill (selling in a retail business), it may be more cause for concern.

And what about traits? Traits are things you are as opposed to things you know or can do. Traits are usually described in cliches: people-oriented, self-starter, highly motivated, and so on. (These cliches are regularly found in the display ads for executive jobs—I'm not sure they apply to entrepreneurs, who are often described as eccentric.) In any event, there is little you can do to change them and only two seem essential to success:

- *Physical.* You *will* need to have whatever level of health and energy the business and your objectives require.

- *Mental.* Most businesses don't require super intelligence, but you should be alert for special requirements such as the creativity in an advertising agency or the fashion sense in a business involving style or design.

The Myth of the Entrepreneurial Type

Now a few words about comparing yourself with entrepreneurs. You've probably heard the stereotypical descriptions of entrepreneurs. The descriptions are so exaggerated you would bet you could recognize one of these superhumans on sight. (Most likely by the glint in the eye and the brash, self-assured walk.) There are tests that can compare you to the profile of a successful entrepreneur.* The profiles exhibit a remarkable similarity to the profile of *any* successful businessperson. That shouldn't be surprising. Good work habits, tenacity, a solid sense of self, and reasonable risk taking are always valuable traits, and little is ever accomplished without strong desire. But like any successful group of business people, entrepreneurs have traits that range from shy to pugnacious, from workaholic to sloth, and from vivacious to dull as a stone. Some were previous failures and some have been winners at everything they've tried. Some are driven by insecurity and others can't even imagine failure.

There are extreme definitions of entrepreneurs which restrict the term to the creators of new enterprises. Other definitions are broad enough to include anyone who bears the ultimate risk of a business. It's important to put this idea of the successful entrepreneurial type in perspective. There are no easy checklists that can eliminate or excuse you from considering your own business or that can guarantee you have the "right stuff." Other than strong desire, there is no special common denominator.

What It All Means

After you have thoroughly reviewed your knowledge, skills, and traits, reflect on your analysis from Worksheet 5. How do you look on paper?

*Those who want to conduct a more in-depth personal assessment can obtain self-scoring profile questionnaires from: The American Entrepreneurs Association, 2311 Pontius Avenue, Los Angeles, CA 90064 and The Center for Entrepreneurial Management, 83 Spring Street, New York, NY 10012.

The answer should matter only to you. After all, there is no right way to look on paper.

Successful entrepreneurs are as varied as any of us. No one of them probably has any more *total* knowledge and skill than you do; it's just that what they do have is very relevant to their business. Besides, as we've said, you can almost certainly acquire any needed knowledge and most skills aren't as hard to master as juggling.

Here are two more reasons not to disqualify yourself yet. First, one kind of knowledge or skill can sometimes be substituted for another. For example, you may not have great face-to-face selling skills, but you may have an exceptional skill at managing salespeople. You may not know all the markets for the product, but you may know how to manufacture it better than most people. You get the idea.

The second reason not to get discouraged is you can usually hire people who do have the knowledge and skills you lack. (You might even hire the former owner.) Hiring to get critical knowledge and skills is common, but there is one risk when you're an owner. If the knowledge and skills are *really* critical and if you are relying nearly 100 percent on someone else, you can become a hostage to that employee.

In summary, get a good feel for your knowledge and skills. Be prepared to rule out situations that are obviously outside your competence, but keep the gates as wide open as possible for now. This inventory of knowledge, skills, and traits is where you end up when you use the conventional elements to determine what kind of business you should buy.

Any business description based on these elements will directly reflect your past experience and be very general. That's fine for the moment. Whatever definition you have formed has properly eliminated some extremes and is based on a degree of logic.

Setting Your Criteria

Now let's look at some specific, less conventional criteria which can truly trigger a positive or negative response to a business opportunity. These are the things we really think about when we evaluate a business. As personal as it might be, it's time to look at how much money you want to make. First understand clearly the difference between how much money you need and how much money you want.

How Much Money You Need

The temptation here is to add up how much you're spending and say that's how much you need. The fact is, you can always cut back. Cutting back can vary from eliminating some luxury to completely redoing your lifestyle. Do a zero-based budget. Examine everything from the private schools to the how often you go to the movies. Only you can say whether you really need something. You may find it useful to prepare two budgets, one you would like to have and one that represents an absolute minimum.

You should know that some business buyers have had such a strong desire and commitment that they have sold everything and lived with just the barest essentials in order to keep their needs for money low. You should also know when you own your own business, there are ways to shift certain insurance, automobile, legal, accounting, and other expenses to the business. If the business is successful, it can provide employment and perks for family members.

Speaking of family members and money, this is as good a place as any to bring up the subject of how your family fits into this entire process of leaving your job and buying a business. This book isn't intended to be a text on family relations, but this advice is offered. You can understand that your family is going to react with some surprise and anxiety when you tell them what you are considering. If you are the principal wage earner, their concerns will be heightened.

When you explain your desire and explain that this is what you want, their self-concerns can become touched with guilt. You need to help them open up about their concerns. To the extent you honestly can, involve them in the decision. Have them participate in completing the worksheets. Share with them your expectations about how all of you, and your lifestyle, are going to be affected. Talk with them about money, family time, and the stresses to be expected. Share your vision of the opportunity and what it could mean to all of you. Above all, explain the risks as you see them. If you want their support and help, ask for it, particularly if this is the first time they have been involved in your business dealings. You should pay attention to their concerns and they should pay attention to how much you want to do this.

Be as accurate as you can when you decide how much money you need. It is a critical factor in the final decision to buy or not buy a business. If you've overstated how much you need, you may miss a great opportunity. If you understate your needs, you could buy a business and end up in financial distress. Use Worksheet 6A.

How Much Money You Want

This single factor can be the most definitive screening criteria you have. For example, if you want a business that earns a minimum of $500,000 today, you have eliminated all but a few individual retail businesses and nearly any business that you could buy for less than $2 million.

How much money you want to earn has the added dimension of time and can't be totally separated from your other criteria. Here are four examples to demonstrate:

1. You just want to find a company that will provide you with a nice living, year after year. If the business does well, you'll probably trade off any higher earnings to work less instead.

2. You want a company with a present cash flow adequate to cover your needs, but it has to be able to grow. Your targets are $100,000 in 3 years and $200,000 in 5 years. After that, who knows?

3. You don't even care if the business is losing money right now. What you want is a business that can grow into a multimillion dollar enterprise. Without that potential, you aren't going to give up your present situation.

4. It really depends on what you're doing. If you can find a business in the perfect location, involved in your favorite area of interest, or one that satisfies your criteria for status, travel, etc., the money you want is relatively unimportant.

In fact, you're probably somewhere in between these examples.

What's important right now is to convert your income desires into criteria against which you can measure the business you are going to consider. Use Worksheet 6B.

Now that you have set criteria to cover how much money you need and want, let's start on other criteria.

Location

This simplest of criterion needs to be considered in two ways to determine whether the location suits you (search criterion) and whether it suits the business (evaluation criterion).

Search Criterion. The three general models are:

1. You want businesses only within a commute of your present home.

2. You're willing to relocate anywhere (or somewhere) for the right business.

3. You want to relocate to some specific area.

Buyers are tempted to look at every good opportunity, no matter where it is. You might ask what the harm is in doing so. The harm is that it takes time and effort from you, the seller, and your advisors. Good brokers, for example, will be less inclined to bring opportunities to you if they feel you waste their time by looking at businesses you will never really pursue.

Evaluation Criterion.   Here we are concerned about whether the location is a plus or minus for the specific business you are considering. Each business will have different needs for street visibility, traffic, parking, ease of access, neighborhood surroundings, proximity of competition, and labor availability.

Mention should be made here about the risk of moving a business that you buy. It is a potentially costly proposition. You may lose key employees, customers, vendors, and community relationships. The new buyer of a business has plenty to contend with already. Some businesses can be moved and others should be moved, but most should be left where they are, at least until you establish yourself in the business. Use Worksheet 6C.

Risk

This is the most complex of the criteria to establish. Risk has many dimensions, one of which needs special explanation.

Risk Preference.   This dimension of risk is called "risk preference." The easiest way to understand it is through an analogy with flipping a coin. The odds when flipping a coin are 50/50 no matter how much I bet. I'm comfortable when I bet a dollar or two, but I would never bet a thousand dollars. I prefer not to risk that much even though the odds are still the same and I might still double my money. Some people prefer to invest very little in high-risk/high-return ventures; others prefer these types of ventures as investments. Any investment has this phenomenon attached to it, and unless you are aware of it, you might not be able to communicate your criteria of risk.

Risk of Loss.   The more well-known dimensions of risk are the risk of losing your investment and the risk of not earning a return on your investment. (Return is not only the earnings on the investment but the appreciation in value of the investment as well.)

Buying a business with lots of readily salable assets (a machine shop with standard equipment or a liquor store with normal inventory) provides a lower risk *of* your investment than businesses like advertising agencies or real estate firms, which have few assets. However, the machine shop and the liquor store are rather fixed in the ways they can earn a return *on* your investment and therefore are more risky in this dimension than the advertising agency and real estate firm, which have wider ranges of earning behavior and less fixed expense to carry.

Here is one last thing to consider when thinking about risk. If you plan to manage the business you are going to buy, you are also risking your time. Remember, we are not calculating rates of return or computing your probability of success in a specific business yet; we are establishing your criteria regarding risk. Even assuming that you and your advisors will structure the purchase as best you can to limit risks, you must prepare yourself to take some degree of risk.

In summary, then, you have *assets* and *time* you are preparing to invest for a *return*. There is no mathematical formula to set this criteria, but you should develop qualitative descriptions of the degree of risk you are prepared to take. Use Worksheet 6D.

Liquidity

Unlike risk, this is a straightforward issue. How quickly could the business be converted to cash? No business provides the liquidity of stocks, bonds, or other similar investments, but some businesses have more liquidity than others. The distribution businesses with stock being held on consignment can be converted to cash easily; the rental apartment complex may take many months.

Once again, we are not yet evaluating businesses, just establishing your criteria for liquidity. You should determine if you are liable to face any sudden obligations or investment opportunities requiring cash. If you don't provide for your cash needs, you could be forced to sell assets or your entire company under "fire-sale" conditions. Use Worksheet 6E.

Growth Potential

This is a very useful criteria because it is a very good screen. If you require a "sky's-the-limit" type of business, you are not going to want a historic bed and breakfast inn on the sea coast of Maine. This is not to say a business that is small today can't be expanded. That's the very essence of potential. Many businesses can be expanded physically, geographically, and conceptually. In fact, almost any business can be grown to some extent. The practical facts are some businesses lend themselves to growth through easy replication, fast-growing markets, or competitive advantage, while others do not. Your task is to decide what you need for growth potential in the business you are going to buy. Use Worksheet 6F.

Physical and Other Working Conditions

Most of us can be somewhat flexible in this area, but make sure you know your limits. A screw machine shop can require 12 hours a day in the factory, a wine distributorship can mean 5 days a week on the road, and owning a company which consults on fund-raising could easily lead to 4 nights a week attending meetings.

To some buyers, predictable hours which allow for family or hobbies is an important criteria. Some buyers feel they are at a stage at which comfortable surroundings do matter. On the other hand, some may be willing to work nights and weekends from a briefcase in the corner of a warehouse.

One aspect of working conditions can be quantified. You can calculate what a luxurious office suite, plush furniture, and a private secretary cost. In metropolitan centers, the costs could exceed $50,000 per year:

800 square feet at $25 per foot	$20,000
Private secretary	30,000
$10,000 furnishing (5-year life)	2,000
Total	$52,000

No matter where you are on the scale, the physical environment and working conditions of your new company are important components of your future satisfaction. Use Worksheet 6G.

Status and Image

This is a very personal issue. When buying a business, you should be excited about seeing yourself as the owner. Some people would rather own a break-even newspaper than a very profitable, high-volume gas station/convenience store. For some people, the business will have to be large; for others it will need to be glamorous. There is no right or wrong in such a personal arena. Just be sure you honestly match the business to your needs for status and image. Use Worksheet 6H.

People Intensity

"The more people, the more problems," say many business owners. People problems can result from the difficulty in managing a large work force. Ask the owner of a big real estate company or the night-shift manager of an industrial cleaning business.

But people problems can also result from a lack of workers to fill job openings. In Fairfield County, Connecticut, for example, workers for fast food stores, supermarkets, and shopping centers are being bussed in from surrounding counties. A lack of affordable housing may perpetuate this situation for some time.

If the business is dependent on the number and quality of the people you can attract and retain, you need to be comfortable managing people. To some buyers, this is an important criterion of the business. Use Worksheet 6I.

Competitive Environment

No business is completely without competition, but there are extremes. At one end are businesses in large markets that face competition everywhere. Food service is an example. In any market there are restaurants, fast food franchises, deli's, and even supermarkets, all competing for the business. At the other extreme are special-niche businesses in relatively small markets. A company that makes turntables for revolving restaurants is an example of this kind of business. If the extent of competition is important to you, make it a part of your search criteria. Use Worksheet 6J.

Specific Business Content

You may have special requirements for your business. Perhaps it has to be involved in some specific field so you can capitalize on your experience. Maybe it has to serve some social goal. You may want a manufacturing business, or you may want to exclude restaurants. You might want to be involved in or avoid high technology, international dealings, or some other special element of business. The point is, if something is important to you, make it a part of your business criteria.

This criterion is really at the heart of determining what kind of business you want. Spend a lot of time on it. It's going to be the key starting point in your search for a business. The following are suggestions on how to establish this criterion.

Don't Be Afraid to Dream. This is the time to consider what you really want to do with your life. Go beyond the obvious:

An executive who loves to cook might make a lousy restaurateur but might publish a great newsletter on kitchen appliances and utensils.

A pet fancier might never be able to become a veterinarian but could own a boarding kennel or grooming salon or a chain of them.

If the outdoor life is for you, you don't have to become a forest ranger. There are tree service companies, fishing lodges, lawn, landscaping and yard care firms, fencing companies, and many others.

If sports are important in your life, you can look for a sporting goods store, but how about a small magazine that caters to some special sports niche?

For those who want world travel, a travel agency will do it, but why not look for an import/export business?

Owning a business in a field you love is no guarantee you will be good at it, but the added enthusiasm that comes from doing something you thoroughly enjoy can help you succeed.

Don't Be Too Rigid.   While you may initially determine you want a manufacturing company, remember this is only one of your criteria. At this stage, you aren't even aware of the many kinds of businesses which exist and might really make you happy. If you have never worked with the Standard Industrial Classification (SIC) system, you should review the descriptions in this most widely used method of classifying businesses (see Appendix A). Just reviewing the names of these business types can spark ideas. Your local Yellow Pages are another source of ideas.

Don't Think You Have to Get What You Want All at Once.   If you want to own a large commercial printing firm, you might start off by owning a small quick-print shop. You may want a telecommunications company, and you could get started by buying a small interconnect business or an answering service.

The important thing is to get into the arena you want; then you can get familiar with the market, the suppliers, the competitors, and the customers. This is how you'll find the next opportunity and build the base to take advantage of it. Use Worksheet 6K.

Summary

Here are some of the things you should think about when deciding what kind of business you want:

- *Your knowledge and skills.* While you should eliminate businesses for which you truly have no base of competence, you can, at a cost, acquire or hire most knowledge and skill.

- *Your traits.* Other than the basic physical and mental requirements, there are no magic common denominators you must have or lack.

- *How much money you need.* It's up to you. You can live in a tent and have the kids work their way through college, or you can maintain a high standard. We recommend a two-level personal budget.

- *How much money you want.* Again, it's up to you. Just keep in mind the dimensions of time and the trade-off with other criteria.

- *Location.* If it's important, say so.

- *Risk.* It's not only the risk of your investment and your time; it's the type of risk you prefer.

- *Liquidity.* If you think you may need your cash in a hurry, choose a business that you can liquidate easily, or you can be forced to sell cheap.

- *Growth potential.* There are lots of ways to grow. If growth is important, be sure the potential is there.

- *Physical working conditions.* Make certain you can put up with the hours required and the conditions under which you'll be working.

- *Status and image.* For some people, ownership of any business is high status; others have more complex status needs. Know yours.

- *People intensity.* Whether it's managing people or simply finding enough of them, be prepared for problems if you are considering businesses which have lots of people.

- *Competition.* Some love it; some hate it. Whatever your criteria, remember this aspect of a business changes only slowly, if at all, and usually for the worse.

- *The content of the business.* This is the heart of it. Be flexible, take bite-size chunks, and give some creative thought to a business based in some field which will give you great personal satisfaction.

Worksheets 6A through 6K will help you organize the information to set your criteria. The worksheets can be used later to rate your candidate company against the criteria.

Worksheet 5
Personal Inventory

A. KNOWLEDGE—THINGS YOU KNOW
   What five things do you know more about than almost anybody?
   1. _____
   2. _____
   3. _____
   4. _____
   5. _____

   And less about?
   1. _____
   2. _____
   3. _____
   4. _____
   5. _____

B. SKILLS—THINGS YOU CAN DO
   What five things can you do better than almost anybody?
   1. _____
   2. _____
   3. _____
   4. _____
   5. _____

   And less well?
   1. _____
   2. _____
   3. _____
   4. _____
   5. _____

C. TRAITS—THINGS YOU ARE
   I am . . .
   1. _____
   2. _____
   3. _____
   4. _____
   5. _____

   I am not . . .
   1. _____
   2. _____
   3. _____
   4. _____
   5. _____

D. WHAT THE INVENTORY MEANS
   The inventory suggests I should consider these kinds of business/situations:
   1. _____
   2. _____
   3. _____

   And avoid these:
   1. _____
   2. _____
   3. _____

N.B. If your spouse or another family member will be part of this effort at business ownership, repeat the form for him or her.

Worksheet 6
Setting Your Criteria

Complete the top portion of each criterion in Worksheet 6 now and save it. Complete the bottom portion, rating your candidate company, once you find one, from 1 to 10 (10 is best).

A. HOW MUCH MONEY YOU NEED

Item	Minimum Amount	Desired Amount
Housing (primary home)	$ _____	$ _____
Utilities	_____	_____
Transportation	_____	_____
Food (in home)	_____	_____
Meals (outside of home)	_____	_____
Clothing	_____	_____
Education	_____	_____
Entertainment/vacations	_____	_____
Medical & hygiene expenses (est.)	_____	_____
Life insurance	_____	_____
Health insurance	_____	_____
Other insurance	_____	_____
Dues, memberships, donations	_____	_____
Maintenance, cleaning, laundry	_____	_____
Debt repayments	_____	_____
Savings	_____	_____
Other	_____	_____
Other	_____	_____
Total	$ _____	$ _____

Company ratings:
Your candidate company has an estimated cash flow available to an owner of $ _____ . Your candidate company rates _____ .
                                        (1 to 10)

N.B.   Be sure you are comparing your needs and the candidate's cash flow on the same tax basis.

B.   HOW MUCH MONEY YOU WANT
     Consider amount, growth, and risk.
     Year 1 $ _____   Year 3 $ _____   Year 5 $ _____
     Year 2 $ _____   Year 4 $ _____

     Company rating:
     You estimate that your candidate company can provide:
     Year 1 $ _____   Year 3 $ _____   Year 5 $ _____
     Year 2 $ _____   Year 4 $ _____

     Your candidate company rates _____ .
                                        (1 to 10)

C.   LOCATION
Search criterion:
1.   Must be within _____ miles.
2.   Can be in _____ or _____ .
3.   Can be anywhere; I will move.
4.   I am prepared to relocate the business if I have to.

Evaluation Criterion: Consider visibility, traffic, parking, ease of access, neighborhood surroundings, proximity of competition, and labor availability.

Company rating:
Your candidate company location is _____ .
Your candidate company rates _____ .
                                        (1 to 10)

Worksheet 6 continued

D. RISK PREFERENCE

For an acceptable opportunity:
I am prepared to risk $ _____ in total, with $ _____ down payment and _____ years of work.

For an excellent opportunity:
I am prepared to risk $ _____ in total, with $_____ down payment and _____ years of work.

Assuming a typical business opportunity with a normal degree of risk, I can mark myself on this scale:

I will risk some of my savings but not my house or other possessions.	I will risk it all to have my own business.

Company rating:
Your candidate company requires $ _____ in total, with $ _____ down payment and a potential commitment of _____ years.

Your candidate company rates _____ .
                                        (1 to 10)

E. LIQUIDITY

	Annual Cash Requirements		
Year	Known*	Probable	Possibile
1	$ _____	$ _____	$ _____
2	_____	_____	_____
3	_____	_____	_____
4	_____	_____	_____
5	_____	_____	_____

*This amount can come from Worksheet 6A, "How much money you need." If you face sudden requirements for cash, your business needs to be easily able to be converted to cash or to be sold.

Company rating:

Year	Estimated Cash Flow from Normal Operations	Estimated Additional Cash Available through Liquidation of Assets	Total
Historical average	$ _____	N/A	$ _____
1	_____	$ _____	_____
2	_____	_____	_____
3	_____	_____	_____
4	_____	_____	_____
5	_____	_____	_____

Your candidate company rates _____ .
                                        (1 to 10)

F. GROWTH POTENTIAL

My basic objective is to live well. If (when) the business has sales of $ _____ and an owner's cash flow of $ _____ , all I will want is enough growth to keep the business healthy.

I eventually want a business with sales of approximately $ _____ and an owner's cash flow of about $ _____ . The business I buy needs to be capable of reaching that level in _____ years.

My objective is to build a very large company very quickly. Any business I buy must have at least $ _____ in sales and $ _____ in owner's cash flow now and in five years should have $ _____ in sales and $_____ in owner's cash flow.

Worksheet 6 continued

Company rating:

Your candidate company is estimated to have this growth potential:

Year	Sales	Owner's Cash Flow
Present Level	$ _____	$ _____
1	_____	_____
2	_____	_____
3	_____	_____
4	_____	_____
5	_____	_____

Your canidate company rates _____
(1 to 10)

G.   PHYSICAL WORKING CONDITIONS:

The hours per week I want to work _____ .

The number of days per month I want to travel _____ .

The type of office or surroundings I want can best be described as _____ .

It is _____ is not _____ important that I avoid certain hazardous or physical conditions.

Company rating:

Your candidate company has these characteristics:

Working hours per week _____

Days travel per month _____

Office/surroundings that can be described as _____

Hazardous or dangerous conditions wich include _____

Your candidate company rates _____
(1 to 10)

H.   STATUS AND IMAGE

I want:	No	Doesn't Matter	Yes
A business which will give me high visibility.	_____	_____	_____
A business which is considered large or substantial.	_____	_____	_____
A business which is more knowledge based (white collar) than skill based (blue collar).	_____	_____	_____
A business involved in a sophisticated or glamorous field.	_____	_____	_____
A business on the cutting edge of innovation.	_____	_____	_____
A business which provides a service to the community and its people.	_____	_____	_____

Company rating:

Your candidate company:	Yes	No
Will give high visibility	_____	_____
Is considered large or substantial	_____	_____
Is a "white collar" business	_____	_____
Is sophisticated/glamorous	_____	_____
Is on the cutting edge of innovation	_____	_____
Provides community or other service	_____	_____

Your candidate company rates _____ .
(1 to 10)

Worksheet 6 continued

I. PEOPLE INTENSITY:
    People Issue

	My Degree of Comfort	
	Low	High
Recruiting, interviewing, hiring, training	_____	_____
Specialized skills supervision	_____	_____
Wage and salary administration	_____	_____
Union (labor) relations	_____	_____
Personnel policy development and administration	_____	_____
"Motivation," discipline, firing	_____	_____
Organization design and development	_____	_____
Conflict resolution, counseling	_____	_____
Recognition and incentives	_____	_____
High turnover, morale problems	_____	_____
OSHA, ERISA, etc.	_____	_____

Company rating:
Your candidate company:

	Required Degree of Intensity	
People Situation	Low	High
Recruiting, interviewing, hiring, training	_____	_____
Specialized skills supervision	_____	_____
Wage and salary administration	_____	_____
Union (labor) relations	_____	_____
Personnel policy development and administration	_____	_____
"Motivation," discipline, firing	_____	_____
Organization design and development	_____	_____
Conflict resolution, counseling	_____	_____
Recognition and incentives	_____	_____
High turnover, morale problems	_____	_____
OSHA, ERISA, etc.	_____	_____

Your candidate company rates _____ .
                        (1 to 10)

J. COMPETITIVE ENVIRONMENT

	Yes	No
It is important that the business I buy is the only business (or one of the only business) of its type in the market area.	_____	_____
The business I buy must be the market-share leader or near leader in its field.	_____	_____
I want a business with high barriers to entry for potential competitors.	_____	_____
I especially want protections such as patents and licenses.	_____	_____
The business should not be subject to inordinate foreign competition.	_____	_____
The business must measure up to competitors in terms. of margins, productivity, modern equipment, etc.	_____	_____

Company rating:
Your candidate company:
         Has _____ competitors in its market.
         Has _____ percent market share and ranks no._____ .
         Is in a field with high _____ low _____ barriers to entry.
         Has patents or licenses: yes _____ no _____ .
         Is subject to inordinate foreign competition: yes _____ no _____ .
         Has competitive margins, productivity, equipment, etc.: yes _____ no _____ .
Your candidate company ranks _____
                        (1 to 10)

Worksheet 6 continued

K. SPECIFIC BUSINESS CONTENT:
    The three things I have most enjoyed doing:
    In my business career:
    1. _____
    2. _____
    3. _____

    As family or recreational activities:
    1. _____
    2. _____
    3. _____

    In academic pursuits:
    1. _____
    2. _____
    3. _____

    In community or public service:
    1. _____
    2. _____
    3. _____

    As fantasies:
    1. _____
    2. _____
    3. _____

    Based on these most enjoyed activities and on my knowledge, skills, and traits, here are some kinds of businesses that either make, service, sell, consult, or are in some way a possible fit for me:

    _____
    _____
    _____
    _____
    _____
    _____

    My "perfect company" would be:

    _____
    _____
    _____

Company rating:
What your candidate company does:

    _____
    _____
    _____

What it could do:

    _____
    _____
    _____

Your candidate company rates _____ .
                              (1 to 10)
N.B.   If your spouse or another family member will be a part of this effort at business ownership, repeat form for him or her.

4

Determining What You Can Afford

Before you begin your search for a business, which is coming up in the next chapter, it is helpful to have an idea of what you can afford. You don't want to waste your time pursuing businesses which are beyond your means or miss out on businesses which you can afford. Unfortunately, you will only have a general idea of what you can afford at the outset because so much will depend on the specific company and on the final terms of the purchase. What you can afford is contingent on four things:

The value (price) of the business and the terms of sale

How much money you have or can borrow

Your ability to persuade lenders or investors

The capacity of the business to support itself, support you, and repay its debt

You may be surprised at what you can afford.

The Value (Price) of the Business and the Terms of Sale

Valuing businesses is done by methods ranging from crude rules of thumb (x times cash flow) to exotic and intricate mathematical models.

Worksheet 7 is included at the end of this chapter to help you value and price your candidate company. The following two organizations have members who specialize in valuing businesses:

The Institute of Business
Appraisers, Inc.
P.O. Box 1447
Boynton Beach, FL 33435

The Business Valuation Committee
of the American Society of
Appraisers
publishers of *Business Valuation Review*
P.O. Box 24222
Denver, CO 80224

Individual appraisers specializing in machinery, professional practices, real estate, and other classifications can be found in most yellow pages. In addition, many books have been published on the subject of appraisal and valuation of businesses (see Appendix E).

The degree and depth of your evaluation will depend on how much you feel you need. If you are buying a large company with substantial assets and real estate, you may want a professional evaluation. The purchase of a small service or retail company may require no more than a common-sense idea of value.

Comparisons Are Not Valid

One method of valuation *not* available to you as a business buyer is the method which uses comparisons of one business with others. This is the common way to determine the price of residential real estate where the recent selling prices on nearly identical houses in similar locations is known. Businesses are not similar enough to compare and the selling prices are not published as are the prices for real property.

The Three Components of Value

Whether the evaluation is highly detailed or very basic, it involves three elements:

What a business owns—usually found on the balance sheet

What a business earns—the profit/cash flow

What makes the business unique—the degree of risk

Each of these elements has a value and the three can be combined in some very surprising ways.

A company with a factory full of equipment is making something the market no longer wants and the cost of retooling is prohibitive. It has $10 million in sales, but it had to cut price to get the volume and it lost $1 million last year. So far we have a company with lots of assets and $10 million in sales, but the assets are outdated and the cash flow from the sales is negative. If, however, the company is your only competitor, its value to you could be very high.

An example of the reverse combination might be the gas station that has few assets and rather modest sales but earns its owner over $250,000 a year because it is the only station on the road between two distant towns. Unfortunately, a new super highway which will connect the two towns is being built 3 miles east of the present road.

There are two points to these examples:

- Relying on just the quantitative value of each element can be misleading.
- Relying on less than all the elements can be misleading.

While it would take extensive formal training to make you a professional appraiser, the following material should provide you with useful knowledge of the concepts.

What a Business Owns

The "balance sheet" is a useful indicator of value. It is basically a statement showing what a company owns (assets) less what it owes (liabilities) and the remaining balance (net worth) according to certain accounting rules. Balance sheets can look very complicated and may require professional advice to interpret the implications of the items and their treatment.* They do not automatically indicate the value or price of the business. Assets are generally stated at historic cost less allowances for depreciation, not at current value. Replacement values may be higher or lower than the stated cost.

Here are some examples which show the limitations of the balance sheet:

*This book is not an accounting text. For a quick, basic understanding of accounting and its terms we recommend several books in Appendix E.

	Company A	Company B
Cash	$ 20,000	$ 15,000
Accounts receivable	85,000	40,000
Inventory	100,000	65,000
Total current assets	205,000	120,000
Property, plant, & equipment	600,000	750,000
Less depreciation	(100,000)	(500,000)
Net fixed assets	500,000	250,000
Total assets	705,000	370,000
Accounts payable	65,000	60,000
Short-term note	50,000	40,000
Total current liabilities	115,000	100,000
Long-term debt	290,000	170,000
Total liabilities	405,000	270,000
Simple net worth	300,000	100,000

Company A would seem a much stronger and more valuable company until we apply the two tests that are important to the buyer:

1. *What are the assets really worth at fair market value?* As a buyer, lender, or investor you are really interested in the market value of the assets. Cash, accounts receivable, inventory, and other current assets are relatively easy to test for market value. (Chapter 7 will cover how to examine the business.) The fixed assets can present a problem.

In our example, Company A rents its facility and has all new equipment which could be sold to others for about what is shown on the balance sheet. The market value of Company A's fixed assets is close to the depreciated book value shown on the balance sheet. Company B, on the other hand, has older equipment that has been depreciated and it owns its own factory. The equipment has been well maintained and is worth more than its depreciated value. More importantly, Company B's real estate, which is on the books for the original cost of the land plus the depreciated cost of the building, is in a high-value area and is worth $2 million at today's market price.

The point to remember is the accounting balance sheet alone is not enough to determine the real value of the assets.

2. *What do these assets earn for the business?* Some assets, like specialized machinery, may have little market value but might produce

products that earn high profit. Excess inventory, on the other hand, may technically have market value but may cost a company more interest costs and spoilage to carry than it will earn when it eventually sells. In the case of our two examples, let's assume that Company A operates at a substantial loss. This means that even though the assets on the balance sheet are valuable, they aren't doing Company A any good and might better be liquidated.

The point here is for assets to have value to a business, they need to earn money.

What a Business Earns

"Profit and cash performance" is the second key indicator of a company's value and another case in which isolated analysis is misleading. The profit on the accounting statement has to first be adjusted to show the owner's real cash flow. Then the adjusted cash flow is measured as a return on the investment tied up in the business.

Business owners, particularly those who run small businesses, often treat income and expenses in ways which minimize their total taxes. They may over- or underpay themselves. They may lavish prerequisites on themselves and their families or they may have everyone working for nothing. They may make substantial reinvestments in the business, but treat them as expenses.

These and other practices, if identified, need to be adjusted in order to show a true picture of the business' performance. The rule is simply to determine the true required cost and adjust accordingly.

Adjusted Owner's Cash Flow. Our definition of "adjusted owner's cash flow" is the cash available to an owner after adjusting expenses to the required level and after allowing an appropriate salary for the owner's effort in the business. This adjusted owner's cash flow is calculated with no allowance for interest or depreciation; that is, any interest or depreciation is added back as a plus to cash flow. The result is cash available to the owner for reinvestment, growth, taxes, debt repayment, or dividends.

The adjusted income statement below is a fairly typical example of a small business in which the owner has taken a larger salary and more benefits than would be truly required if a paid manager were used. The happy outcome here is an adjusted cash flow of $82,000 in excess of the stated profit.

	Per statement	True required cost	Adjustment
Sales	$500,000	$500,000	0
Cost of goods sold	200,000	200,000	0
Gross profit	$300,000	$300,000	0
Expenses:			
Employee salaries	$100,000	$100,000	0
Employee benefits	25,000	25,000	0
Owner/manager's salary	75,000	30,000	+$ 45,000
Owner/manager's benefits	11,000	5,000	+ 6,000
Travel/entertainment	15,000	5,000	+ 10,000
Rent	15,000	15,000	0
Utilities and telephone	12,000	10,000	+ 2,000
Selling expenses	5,000	5,000	0
Insurance	8,000	7,000	+ 1,000
Automobile	9,000	0	+ 9,000
Legal/accounting	12,000	6,000	+ 6,000
Donations	3,000	0	+ 3,000
Total expenses	$290,000	$208,000	+ $ 82,000
Income before interest, depreciation, reinvestment, and taxes	$ 10,000		
Adjustments			+ $ 82,000
Cash available		$ 92,000	

This next adjusted statement is also typical, but the outcome is not a happy one.

	Per statement	True required cost	Adjustment
Sales	$750,000	$750,000	0
Cost of goods sold	450,000	450,000	0
Gross profit	300,000	$300,000	0
Expenses:			
Employee salaries	150,000	$150,000	0
Employee benefits	0	36,000	− $ 36,000
Owner/manager's salary	0	30,000	− 30,000
Owner/manager's benefits	0	6,000	− 6,000
Travel/entertainment	8,000	7,000	+ 1,000
Rent	12,000	32,000	− 20,000
Utilities and telephone	12,000	12,000	0
Selling expenses	0	12,000	− 12,000
Insurance	7,000	7,000	0
Automobile	0	0	0
Legal/accounting	8,000	8,000	0
Donations	0	0	0
Total expenses	$197,000	$300,000	− $ 103,000
Income before interest, depreciation, reinvestment, and taxes	$103,000		
Adjustments			− $ 103,000
Cash available		0	

It often happens that the owner of a small business takes no salary even though he or she may work full time at it. In this case the owner also owns the building and charges the business less than fair market rent. Another major adjustment was required because the owner improperly chose to treat the employees as "contractors" and did not provide proper withholding and insurance. Some adjustments require judgment, such as in this case in which the owner was spending nothing on sales and marketing and an adjustment was made to provide $12,000. What appeared to be $103,000 in profit is really a break even in cash flow.

One Year Figures Are Not Enough.   We have shown only examples for 1 year. It is important to see several years, preferably 5. This will provide you the opportunity to spot trends, to identify any nonrecurring expenses or income, and to determine if any single year is exceptionally good or bad.

Some Cash Needs to be Reinvested.   One final note on understanding cash flow has to do with how much cash has to be put back into the business. The cash flow shown above is labeled "before interest, depreciation, reinvestment, and taxes." A growing company requiring large inventory purchases or plant expansion may require far more cash than that being generated from operations. You should know whether this cash can be borrowed from outside or whether it will require your further cash investment. See Chapter 7 for more on cash flow analysis.

Now that we have an understanding of the cash being generated, we need to look at whether that cash flow is good or bad. Simply put, is this a good return on the investment? Merely calculating the percentage return is not enough. We need to know whether this is a good return in light of the risk we are taking.

What Makes the Business Unique?

"Degree of risk" is the third characteristic of the business that will affect its value. All the intangibles that make the business unique are pluses and minuses to establish the degree of risk. No universal scale exists and everyone's risk preference is different. For example, a person with a marketing background might consider a business requiring sophisticated engineering to be a high risk.

Putting personal risk preference aside, there are some measures of risk that do have general application (see Table 4.1). Worksheet 7C will help you with your risk assessment.

We have now examined the three characteristics which affect the value of a company:

Table 4.1. Risk Assessment Table

Factor	Low risk	High risk
Company history.	Long, profitable history.	New or unprofitable history.
The industry segment.	Stable or growing, highly profitable industry.	Erratic growth or decline, unstable, generally unprofitable industry.
Special skills required for success.	No special skills are required.	Highly specialized or scarce skills are required.
Location (or lease term).	The location is excellent and can continue.	The location is unsuitable and/or requires relocation.
Special relationships required for success.	Success is broadly based.	Success depends upon a few key relationships or customers.
Labor situation.	Labor is available and labor relations are good.	Labor is scarce and/or labor relations are poor.
Management situation.	You and/or the remaining management team are fully qualified and competent.	Neither you nor management are competent to run the business.
Return *of* investment.	You would be able to liquidate your investment for about what you paid.	Your investment could be easily depleted or is nonliquid.
Return *on* investment.	Market, economic, and historical factors indicate that returns will continue.	There are no prospects for return without changes in the company, the market, or the economy.
Outside dependency.	Most of the requirements for success are within the company's control.	Success depends on factors such as interest rates, styles and fashions, or foreign sources which are outside the company's control.
Company reputation.	Well recognized and highly respected.	Unknown or poorly regarded.
Products or services.	High value and responsive to market needs.	Poor quality and/or outdated for the market.
Franchises, licenses, insurance, or bonds required.	No special insurance licenses, franchises, or bonds are required.	The business requires hard to obtain or expensive licenses, franchises, insurance, or bonds.
Competition.	Competition is limited.	Competition is intense and/or increasing.
Technology.	The business is not particularly vulnerable to technological changes.	A change in technology could have a major negative impact.

What the business owns—the balance sheet

What the business earns—profit and cash performance

What makes the business unique—the degree of risk

The next step is to convert *value* into *price*. More precisely you need to convert your assessment of value into price.

Pricing the Assets

The asset value on the balance sheet is the least controversial to establish and convert to a price. Most assets can be counted, appraised, or evaluated. As a starting point, price can equal the fair market value. You are going to pay for things you will own and could resell.

In valuing smaller businesses, pay close attention to the notes, both payable and receivable. These are often borrowings between the owner and the company and may best be removed from your transaction. Some assets are not on the balance sheet and not as easy to value. One unusual asset is a lease which is substantially under market rate. The value can be significant. A 5-year lease on 10,000 square feet at $5 per square foot per year when the market rate is $7.50 is worth $2.50 × 10,000 square feet × 5 years, or $125,000.

Unless you plan to move the business and rent out this 10,000 square feet for the profit, you don't have to value the lease. The positive benefit is already reflected in the profit/cash flow which you are going to price next.

Other such intangibles might be the company name, a customer or client list, a patent, special computer systems, or the like. Once again, the easiest way to value these is to view them as being reflected in the profit/cash flow of the business. If these intangible assets really have any value, they will have earned a premium return and you can reflect that value when you put a price on the profit/cash flow. Sometimes sellers insist that these intangibles be assigned a price. We will see later how to structure an offer to satisfy them. Worksheet 7A will help you price the assets.

Pricing the Cash Flow

Putting a price on the profit/cash flow is more art than science. In theory, we are going to *capitalize the cash flow*. That means we will divide the cash flow figure by the percentage of return on investment we think we should earn and so get the price we would pay.

If the cash flow is $100,000 and we want a 25 percent pretax return, we divide $100,000 by 0.25 and find we would invest $400,000 for that stream of cash flow. The task is to select the proper capitalization percent (cap rate). That selection is very dependent upon the degree of risk.

Risk Determines the Capitalization Rate.   Assume that two businesses both have cash flows of $100,000. One is a low-risk business on which you would be satisfied to earn a 20 percent return while the other is a higher-risk business on which you would want a 30 percent return. You would be willing to pay $500,000 ($100,000 divided by 0.20 percent) for the low-risk cash flow but only $333,333 ($100,000 divided by 0.30 percent) for the cash flow with the higher risk.

The higher the risk, the higher the cap rate and therefore the lower the (price) investment we would make. We'll use some extreme examples so that you can get the idea.

- A 15-year-old newspaper delivery service has had a solid history of profit/cash flow and earns $100,000.

- A very large restaurant featuring the owner-chef's French menu has produced $150,000 in profit/cash flow in each of its 3 years of operation.

- A specialized design engineering company builds turntables for revolving restaurants and earned $200,000 in cash flow in its first year.

Compare Your Cap Rate with the Market Rate.   Before we try to develop a cap rate for these companies, we should set a benchmark that will give us a practical frame of reference. We can use a top-grade bond. It has low risk, it's very liquid, it requires little or no time to manage, and, at this writing, it earns 9 percent.

Any business you buy has risk, is not liquid, and does take time to manage so you must expect a higher return (cap rate) on that investment.

Investment Growth or Decline.   Our frame of reference needs one other perspective and that is the potential for increase or decrease in the value of our investment. Our top-grade bond isn't going to go up or down much except to adjust for yield. The investment in a business could multiply many fold or be completely wiped out.

Setting Cap Rates.   Now let's set some cap rates on our examples.

The newspaper delivery business has very low risk. It's been around for years, no special skills are needed, and no competition is likely. About the only risk is that the newspaper will find another firm to deliver its papers. There won't be much chance of loss or growth on your investment. Try 20 percent ($100,000 divided by 0.20 percent equals $500,000).

The restaurant has one big risk factor which is the chef-owner. If he leaves when you buy the business, you will have to replace him. This is a special skill. The 3-year age of the business is neither good nor bad. It doesn't guarantee a following, but the equipment is new enough to be sold for a good price. If you're a chef, use 30 percent, if not, 35 percent ($150,000 divided by 0.30 percent equals $500,000) or ($150,000 divided by 0.35 percent equals $429,000).

The design engineering company is a very high-risk situation. It's new, its market is very narrow and hard to influence, and the need for special skills and relationships is high. Its assets, including its round manufacturing building, have little application to anything else. A 40 percent cap rate is not unreasonable ($200,000 divided by 0.40 percent equals $500,000).

These examples, though realistic, were contrived to make the point that degree of risk can have an impact on the cap rate sufficient to cause three business with widely different cash flows to be theoretically priced the same. Worksheet 7B will help you price the cash flow.

Now we have figured out how to price assets and cash flows. If a company had only one or the other, coming up with a total price would be easy. In fact, in a service company, such as one that provides night guards, there may be no assets to speak of and the whole price will be based on the value of the cash flow using the capitalization rate idea. Because many companies do have both assets and cash flow, we need a way to price them together.

Integrated Pricing

One method which values assets and cash flow in an integrated way is called the "excess earnings" method. It assigns a portion of the owner's cash flow to cover the cost of carrying the assets. For example, if the assets are valued at $400,000 and it costs 10 percent to borrow money, the first $40,000 of cash flow is viewed as satisfying the return on the investment in assets. Any cash flow over that is considered "excess." This is multiplied by a factor that reflects the degree of desirability (a similar process to dividing by a cap rate) to get the value of the cash flow. This figure is added to the value of the assets to get the total price. Here is a sample calculation:

Asset value	$ 400,000
Prevailing interest rate	× 10%
Cost of carrying assets	40,000
Owner's cash flow	50,000
Less cost of carrying assets	− 40,000
Excess earnings	10,000
Assumed multiplier (uses a 1 to 6 scale to reflect desirability)*	× 3
Value of excess earnings	30,000
Plus value of assets	400,000
Total value of the business	$ 430,000

*The use of a 1 to 6 scale is not arbitrary. Using factors similar to those we used in our analysis of degree of risk, a business that is average in risk and desirability would be rated 3. This multiplying by 3 gives the same result as dividing by a cap rate of 33 percent, which reflects the return most buyers would want on a business with an average degree of risk.

In cases in which the earnings are negative or not enough to carry the cost of the assets, the business is considered to be worth less than even the value of the assets:

Asset value	$400,000
Interest rate	× 10%
Cost of carrying assets	40,000
Owner's cash flow	25,000
Less cost of carrying assets	40,000
Excess earnings (negative)	(15,000)
(Assumed multiplier cannot be used with negative excess earnings.)	
Value of excess earnings	(15,000)
Plus value of assets	400,000
Total value of the business	$385,000

Worksheet 7D will help you perform pricing calculations.

Now that we've spent considerable time on detailed methods of arriving at a price, we will learn that these calculations provide only an approximation and a starting point. The terms of sale and a number of other negotiating issues to be covered in Chapter 8 will affect the final price.

Terms of Sale

What you can afford depends much more on the actual cash required than on the price. The terms of sale can range from all cash at closing to no cash down with payment over several years. All-cash terms should bring about the lowest price but will of course result in the highest cash requirement.

In theory, any all-cash price can be converted to a price involving payment terms over time by using standard payment tables for any specified interest rate.

When calculating the impact of terms on the selling price, four variables are involved: the cash down payment, the length of time for repayment, the interest rate, and whether the payments are fully amortizing or involve a large (balloon) payment at the end of the term. If you work with loan tables and do a few calculations, you will develop a general feel for the impact of certain changes in these variables. Figure 4.1

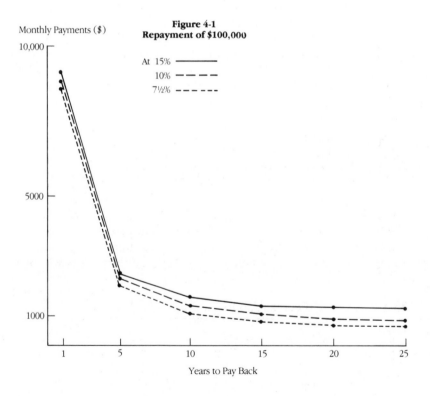

Figure 4.1. Repayment of $100,000 at 7 ½ (.....), 10 (- - - - -), and 15 (———) percent.

and Table 4.2 give you some idea of the impact of trade-offs. It shows clearly that extending the term of a loan to even 5 years reduces monthly payments dramatically. The figure shows why hard bargaining for a point or two of interest or pressing strongly for 20-year terms may earn you less than you concede to achieve them.

In practice, sellers are willing to accept a lower real price for an all-cash transaction and want a premium if they provide extended terms. The sellers of small businesses usually do offer to finance part of the purchase, as we will see.

The Balance Sheet. This can be involved in the terms of sale. Most purchases of small businesses are purchases of assets, not purchases of stock. The buyer pays for the assets and the seller discharges the liabilities. But if the buyer agrees to discharge the liabilities, he or she only pays for the difference between the assets and liabilities, thus requiring less cash to the seller. Of course these liabilities do have to be paid at some time and the creditors often have to agree to the arrangement.

Another way the balance sheet can be used is to arrange, coincidental with your purchase, to borrow against the assets of the business, provided you haven't pledged the assets to the seller. As a frame of reference, banks and others will usually lend on a percentage of value:

Machinery and equipment	50%
Inventory	50%
Accounts Receivable	50–75%

You may be able to borrow against an order backlog or special contract.

Selling assets and then renting or leasing them provides a source of cash. The obvious example is real estate, but machinery, office equipment, and even telephone systems can be leased. If suppliers will pro-

Table 4.2. Monthly Payments to Repay $100,000

Years	7½%	10%	15%
1	8676	8792	9026
5	2004	2125	2379
10	1188	1322	1613
15	928	1075	1400
20	806	965	1316
25	739	908	1280

vide inventory on consignment and allow you to pay for the inventory as you use it and reorder, you can reduce your cash requirement. If there is a patent that makes up a substantial part of the price, you could let the seller keep the patent and instead set up a license to use it and pay a royalty.

Borrowing against assets as a part of the purchase transaction can be coupled with the outright sale of some assets. Unused real estate or an unwanted line of business might be sold to generate cash.

While these ideas on balance sheet financing are valid, they are not appropriate in every situation. The returns you will earn and the basic soundness of your business financing strategy should govern your actions.

Variable, or Contingent, Pricing.   This is the other major concept in setting the terms of sale. Variable pricing is a way to structure terms, not a way to set a price. Using this arrangement, the price established for the business varies in relation to some future event. The most common factor is sales volume. Variable pricing tied to sales can be used when present sales are below historic patterns and the seller claims some unusual event or now-solved problem was responsible. The buyer can agree to some added pay-out schedule if sales materialize at certain levels.

Price can be tied to other variable factors, such as the number of employees who remain with the company for some time (important to real estate firms) or the number of accounts who continue with the company (important to advertising agencies).

Variable pricing can be a powerful way to add to the offered price but keep front-end cash requirements down. Sometimes it is the only method able to provide fairness to both parties. As you see, the terms of sale can have a substantial impact on how much money (cash) you will need.

You should be aware of some other concepts that relate to value, price, and cash needs.

Potential

The first concept has to do with "potential." A business may have few assets and little cash flow, but through either your special skills, some unexploited attribute of the business, or some change in the business' environment, future growth is a high probability.

There are two ways to deal with potential. One is to use the concept of variable pricing presented earlier. Offer to pay more if the growth does, in fact, occur. The opposite view of potential gives it no value or price to the seller. After all, it's the buyer who will do the work, take the risk, make the (possibly substantial) investment, and manage the realization of any potential.

The latter point of view is the more common, but there are plenty of cases in which some event such as the construction of a new highway or the demise of a major competitor just about insures growth with little cost or effort. Either way, you should not normally pay for potential before it is realized.

Duplication Cost

Another concept to apply to the value and price of a business is called duplication cost. The idea is to calculate what it would cost to duplicate the *present* business. The part of the calculation relating to assets and costs is fairly easy. You can price assets in similar condition and you can assume some level of working capital (the difference between current assets and current liabilities). You can get a good idea of prices for real estate and the costs for labor, insurance utilities, and so forth. The problem comes when trying to calculate how long it will take for you to get your new company up to the level of operations and profitability of the company under consideration.

Some companies may be easy to duplicate or even surpass. New businesses, poorly run or badly located businesses, and businesses requiring little know-how are examples. If the company under consideration is efficient, well established, and profitable, it could take years of operation to achieve a similar position. During these years you could suffer low earnings or even losses. And while you might have avoided a high front-end cash investment, you may end up putting as much or more cash into the business.

Duplication cost relates to the concept of the "learning curve" and its impact on efficiency. The assumption is that experience has a value, and there is a cost to obtain it. Before coming to any conclusion about the price of a business you should consider what it would take to duplicate it.

Special Factors of Value

Another concept to consider involves special factors that make the business worth a premium to you. A large backlog of business or an ongoing contract are two examples. Synergy, the elimination of a competitor, obtaining some special license, or even emotional factors may make the business worth a higher price to you.

Be prepared for the seller to ask for some money for "the going business" or "the good will." What the seller means is there should be some price paid for all those intangibles such as the business name and reputation, the customer list, the business systems and controls, and all the other valuable elements which have been assembled over the years.

Your answer should be that you are willing to pay for them and, in fact, you are paying for them if you have offered more than the value of the tangible assets. As mentioned earlier, if all these intangible assets really do have any value, they have been earning income for the business. Whether you capitalized the cash flow or used a pricing method which integrates the value of assets and the value of earnings, you *have* given value for the intangibles. If it pleases the seller, you can call this premium over tangible asset value goodwill or the key or the going business value.

On that subjective note we will conclude for now our work on determining how much money you will need.

How Much Money You Have or Can Borrow

Worksheet 8 can help you organize all the possible sources of money. The place to begin is with the wealth you may be surprised to know you already have.

What You Have

Cash and the near cash available from publicly traded stocks and bonds are the easiest to calculate.

Investments of other types such as rental real estate represent another source of money.

Assignable assets such as notes due you or a time-sharing contract can be converted to cash.

Partnership interests may allow for you to cash in or sell out.

Personal property may represent considerable value you can convert to cash. Some determined people have sold almost everything they own in order to buy or start a business.

A second job is another source of cash used by determined people.

Overtime, freelancing, and moonlighting might provide substantial cash in some cases.

A working spouse, in addition to contributing money, may also be able to provide medical and insurance coverage.

Insurance policies can be a surprising source of cash, particularly if they are older policies. Often they can be liquidated and replaced with new insurance products giving you cash to invest.

Deferred compensation can mean cash in one of two ways. As mentioned in Chapter 1, you may be able to get your deferred compensation awarded early as part of your severance. If this isn't possible, the cash will, at least, be realized later.

Retirement accounts, whether they are company managed, your own IRA and Keogh, or any other type, may have rules which allow you to convert them to cash. Penalties may be involved, but you should at least know the potential availability.

Income from trusts and annuities is an obvious source of cash, but less obvious is the fact that this stream of income may be able to be capitalized and sold, thus giving you a lump sum of cash to invest.

The equity in their homes is the significant cash-yielding asset for most people. Rapid inflation in home values and the eagerness of financial institutions to lend against home equity have made cash readily available to the home owner in the form of equity credit lines, a refinanced first mortgage, or a second mortgage.

What you save is the final source of money you already have. Cutting back on club memberships, entertaining, and other luxuries is a first step, but if you are really committed to raising cash, you should consider a complete reevaluation of your life style.

Once you have added up all the money you already (could) have, it's time to see where you can borrow more.

Where You Can Borrow Personally

First we'll consider your opportunities to borrow money personally.

Friends and family represent a common (if sometimes contentious) source of money. In addition to lending money, friends and family can provide financial support by guaranteeing your borrowings from some other source. Co-signing an auto loan is an example familiar to most of us. In business transactions, your co-signer may have to pledge some specific asset such as the equity in a house. Because you are, in effect, "renting" someone else's wealth to be pledged for you, you should be prepared to pay for this financial support.

Your bank or credit union may extend a personal line of credit.

You may have a *margin or borrowing account* with your stock brokerage firm.

You may be able to borrow against *insurance policies.*

A newly recognized source of borrowing is the *credit card.* Some people receive dozens of unsolicited, preapproved credit card applications. With credit limits ranging from $1000 to $5000, this can represent significant credit. One Hollywood producer claims he produced his academy award winning film with the help of nearly $1 million in credit he had amassed from credit cards.

While there are relatively few sources for personal borrowing, there are a tremendous number of sources of money for businesses. (Appendix E offers extensive sources to locate both investors and lenders.)

Where You Can Borrow through the Business

Banks are the most visible source of money. They lend money directly and indirectly through various guarantee programs. Banks can easily provide you with a description of their loan types and can tell you the criteria of the business borrower they consider their market.

Asset lenders and factors provide money against specific assets of the business. They may take a mortgage or lien on the asset, buy it outright at a discount (accounts receivable), or buy it and lease it back to the company.

The *Small Business Administration* (SBA) is an institution which should be understood by everyone in or considering a small business. It provides loans, loan guarantees, participation loans, and financial assistance. It assists state and local government programs to aid small businesses. It offers special programs to aid minorities. It also provides consulting services, training, government contract assistance, and a library of publications for little or no cost. (A list of SBA offices is contained in Appendix C.)

Other Federal agencies, such as the Veterans Administration, the Department of Housing and Urban Development, and the U.S. Department of Agriculture, offer a variety of programs.

Many *states and some cities* also offer loans, guarantees, and other assistance to small business. The departments responsible for these programs usually come under the heading of economic development, small business development, or commerce. Some states and cities offer special grants or tax considerations to companies which participate in programs to create jobs, provide training, or assist minorities.

Partners are another source of money. Any decision on partnerships should be carefully reviewed by your advisors.

If you own or are buying a franchise, the *franchisor* is a potential lender.

A company's *suppliers,* if they sell on credit, are already lenders in a way. Extending the payment terms can generate money. Some suppliers can offer leases in place of sales as a way to reduce large cash requirements. Regular suppliers may be able to provide inventory on a consignment basis in which you are invoiced only when you replace sold stock.

Even *customers* can be sources of money. They can place orders early which might serve as collateral. They can lend money and accept repayment in goods and services.

A *landlord* might be a source of money. Deferring or forgiving some of your rent may be agreeable if the landlord's alternative is empty space. You may be able to renegotiate the lease to provide for lower rent now during your critical period but higher rent later when you believe you can better afford it. A variation on the idea is a lease tied to some percentage of your sales. Your base rent is lower than it would otherwise be, but if you are successful, the landlord can receive much more than the regular market rent rate. This is common in a shopping center tenant lease.

Insurance companies, foundations, and the use of *barter* are less common sources of money but may be available if your intended business has the characteristics to use them.

Venture capitalists and investment bankers are major sources of money. They lend and invest in companies which may have a relatively high degree of risk so they can earn a higher than average rate of return. Their return may be in the form of interest, stock ownership, or consulting fees, but for many venture capital firms, the objective is to take the venture public. A list of venture capital firms is contained in Appendix E. Most of them have a published statement of their objectives and investment criteria.

In addition, there are *venture groups* around the country which exist to bring investors together with investment opportunities. Some of these groups sponsor monthly luncheons at which an open microphone is used to help those seeking funds and the investors to find each other. (Appendix E also contains a list of venture clubs.)

The seller is the most common source of money for buying a business. Estimates are that 75 to 80 percent of businesses are seller financed and the percentage financed is between one-half and two-thirds of the selling price. Borrowing from the seller is easier, cheaper, and can often be for a longer term than from other sources. Sellers are willing to finance the sale partly because they understand and trust the collateral for the loan, which is the business being sold. Another reason for their willingness is the fact that right now *all* their investment is tied up in the business. Your purchase down payment will be some cash in hand. But the major reason sellers provide financing is to help sell the business and to sell it for more than they would get in an all-cash transaction. Sellers know there are more potential buyers who can successfully operate the business and pay off a loan than there are potential buyers with resources to pay all cash.

How to Persuade Lenders or Investors

An axiom in negotiating and selling is "find out what the other party wants." Common sense says that you are more likely to get what you want if the other party gets what it wants. You are also more able to develop alternatives the more fully you understand someone's true desires. Figure 4.2 will give you an idea of what typical lenders and investors want. The following list explains some common lending terms:

Return on investment. Lenders and investors want to earn a return on their investment. Investors may be satisfied with little or no immediate return because their objective is long-term gain. Lenders usually want an immediate schedule of returns that will cover their cost of money and the risk premium of your loan.

Repayment of principle (Investment). Both lenders' and investors' objectives vary here. Some will want scheduled repayment much like a mortgage, while some will leave their money in your company indefinitely, content with the return they are (or will be) receiving, similar to your credit card lender.

Security. Security can be specific, such as a piece of machinery or the accounts receivable, or it can be general, such as a corporate or per-

Source	With collateral inside business (accounts receivable, machinery, inventory, real estate, etc.)	With collateral outside business (home equity, stocks, insurance policies, etc.)	Unsecured (no collateral)	Percentage of equity (ownership in the new company)
Friends and family	X	X	X	X
Bank	X	X		
Margin or borrowing account		X		
Insurance policies		X		
Credit cards			X	
Asset lenders/factors	X			
SBA	X	X		
Federal agencies	X	X		
State and city agencies	X	X		
Partners				X
Employees			X	X
Suppliers	X		X	
Customers	X		X	
Landlord			X	
Insurance companies/foundations	X	X		
Venture capitalists	X	X		X
The seller	X	X	X	X

Figure 4.2. Financing matrix.

sonal guarantee. Large, long-established businesses can borrow on a general line of credit while smaller and less creditworthy companies are required to provide more specific security. It is this fact that severely limits a buyer's ability to borrow money from a bank to finance the purchase of a small company which has few real assets to secure the loan.

Equity participation.   Most lenders don't want stock in the companies they finance. They are in the business of lending money. Investors by definition do own stock and are motivated to provide money, whether debt or equity to increase the total value of their investment.

Your task is to learn from your targeted sources what they want for each of the above and to select those that match your objectives and capabilities. Once you know what your sources want, you can develop your presentation to address the issues of ability to repay and the provision of security.

The Application Presentation

Your application for financing may be an informal meeting with the seller or a full business plan presentation to a venture capital firm. In either case you'll need to cover what you plan to do with the business and why you are qualified to do it. Appendix E gives you references to books and publications which can guide you through the development of a business plan.

The Business Plan

A basic business plan outline might look like this:

1. A summary of the present situation
   a. The market(s)
   b. Competition
   c. The economy
   d. Current financial performance
2. An analysis of company strengths and weaknesses
   a. Management/people
   b. Products and services
   c. Facilities and equipment
   d. Financial resources
   e. Market position
   f. Technology
   g. Other departments and issues as appropriate
3. A description of what needs to be done
   a. Opportunities
   b. Threats
   c. Barriers
   d. Resources
4. A plan of action
   a. What will be done
   b. When
   c. By whom
5. Financial projections
   a. Income and expenses
   b. Balance Sheet
   c. Source and application of cash

6. Measurement
   a. How will you measure results
   b. When
   c. What are the criteria of success

Your Personal Qualifications to Succeed

Submit a resume of your education, knowledge, skills, and experience. Point out where your abilities match the needs of the business plan. Prepare a list of references that will be meaningful. List people who can comment favorably on your business judgment, work habits, and reputation. If you can, list people known to your lenders or investors.

One element that is essential to earn financiers' confidence is your commitment. You will need to submit a personal financial statement which shows both your financial status and how much of it you are directing to the venture. Lenders and investors want to see that you believe strongly enough in yourself and your venture that you will fully commit to it.

Summary

If you thought that determining what you can afford was a simple exercise of computing your net worth, you now know it isn't. The principles, examples, and references were presented to give you a broad look at concepts of value, price, and raising money.

The ultimate test of what you can afford is a test for reasonableness, which the Institute of Business Appraisers in its publication *MO-9* calls the "justification of purchase test." After investing the money you have and what you borrow, the business should generate enough cash to cover its operations, service the debt you incur, provide a return on your down payment, and afford you a fair salary for your time. The answer to the test is so dependent on the specific company being considered and on the terms you negotiate that you need to take the next big step—find a business you want and try to buy it.

Worksheet 7
Pricing the Business

A. WHAT THE BUSINESS OWNS (pricing the assets):

Detail of individual asset or liability value adjustments:

Asset or Liability Name	Reason for Adjustment	Value per Statement	Amount of Adjustment (+ or —)	Estimated Market Value
		$ _____	$ _____	$ _____

Worksheet 7 continued

B. WHAT THE BUSINESS EARNS (pricing the cash flow):

The Income (P&L) Statment
for the Period _____ to _____

	Per Statement	Adjustment	Adjusted Figure
Sales	$ _____		
Cost of sales	$ _____		
Gross profit	$ _____		
Expenses:			
Owner's salary	$ _____	$ _____	$ _____
Owner's benefits	_____	_____	_____
Employee salaries (no. of people _____)	_____	_____	_____
Employee benefits	_____	_____	_____
Rent	_____	_____	_____
Utilities	_____	_____	_____
Travel & entertainment	_____	_____	_____
Selling expenses	_____	_____	_____
Depreciation	_____	_____	_____
Insurance	_____	_____	_____
Interest	_____	_____	_____
Automobile	_____	_____	_____
Legal and accounting	_____	_____	_____
Other _____	_____	_____	_____
Other _____	_____	_____	_____
Other _____	_____	_____	_____
Total Expenses	$ _____	$ _____	$ _____
Pretax profit	$ _____	$ _____	$ [_____]

Owner's Cash Flow Calculation

Adjusted profit shown on above financial statement	$ _____
Interest paid on loans	_____
Depreciation	_____
Salaries/wages paid to persons not required in business	_____
Change in rent because of new owner (+ or —)	_____
Expense of previous nonrecurring items (e.g., computers,)	_____

Other adjustments (+ or —)

_____	_____
_____	_____
_____	_____
_____	_____
_____	_____
_____	_____
Adjusted owner's cash flow	$ [_____]

Worksheet 7 continued

C. WHAT MAKES THE BUSINESS UNIQUE (risk assessment):

| | Your Candidate Rank |
Risk Factor	(1 to 6; 6 is low risk)
Company history	_____
The industry segment	_____
Special skills required	_____
Location /lease terms	_____
Special relationships required	_____
Labor situation	_____
Management situation	_____
Return *of* investment	_____
Return *on* investment	_____
Outside dependency	_____
Company reputation	_____
Products or services	_____
Franchises, licenses, insurance, or bonds required	_____
Competition	_____
Technology	_____
Total	_____

Divide total by 15 for overall risk assessment
(This is also known as the desirability multliplier).

D. PRICING CALCULATIONS
Market value of assets $ _____
Less : liabilities being assumed   — _____
    Price based on assets $ _____

Adjusted owner's cash flow $ _____
Divided by: capitalization rate   _____
    (the rate of return you want on this business)
    Price based on capitalization of cash flow $ _____

Cost to buy assets at market value $ _____
Plus: start-up costs as follows:

Year	Business Losses		Lost Earnings		Annual Costs
1	$ _____	+	$ _____	=	$ _____
2	_____	+	_____	=	_____
3	_____	+	_____	=	_____
4	_____	+	_____	=	_____
5	_____	+	_____	=	_____
N	_____	+	_____	=	_____
Total	$ _____	+	$ _____	=	$ _____

Price based on duplication $ _____

Worksheet 7 continued

Integrated method

Market value of assets	$ _____
Times: prevailing commercial interest rate	x _____ %
Cost of carrying assets	$ _____
Owner's cash flow	$ _____
Less: cost of carrying assets	— _____
Excess earnings	$ _____
Times: desirability multiplier (from item C)	x _____
Value of excess earnings	$ _____
Plus: market value assets	+ _____

Price based on integrated method $ _____

The candidate company has special value because of some unique advantage it can provide, i.e., cost savings, elimination of competition, a hard-to-obtain franchise or license, a valuable location, etc.

Price premium for special value $ _____

E. PRICING TESTS

Alternative investment test:

The present rate of return on a bank CD	_____ %
Salary you could earn as an employee	$ _____
Compared to:	
Rate of return on candidate company:	
Owner's cash flow divided by proposed selling price	_____ %
Owners's salary and cash flow	$ _____

Worksheet 7 continued

Balance Sheet
as of _____

Assets	Per Statement	Adjustments	Estimated Market Value
Current assets:			
Cash	$ _____	$ _____	$ _____
Accounts receivable	_____	_____	_____
Notes receivable	_____	_____	_____
Inventory	_____	_____	_____
Prepaid expenses	_____	_____	_____
Other	_____	_____	_____
Total current assets	$ _____	$ _____	$ _____
Fixed assets:			
Furniture, fixtures, machinery, & equipment net of depreciation	$ _____	$ _____	$ _____
Land and buildings net of depreciation	_____	_____	_____
Other assets	_____	_____	_____
Total fixed assets	$ _____	$ _____	$ _____
Total assets	$ _____	$ _____	$ _____
Current liabilities:			
Accounts payable	$ _____	$ _____	$ _____
Wages payable	_____	_____	_____
Taxes payable	_____	_____	_____
Interest payable	_____	_____	_____
Notes/leases (current portion)	_____	_____	_____
Services or products owed to customers	_____	_____	_____
Other liabilities	_____	_____	_____
Total current liabilities	$ _____	$ _____	$ _____
Long-term liabilities:			
Notes	$ _____	$ _____	$ _____
Mortgages	_____	_____	_____
Other _____	_____	_____	_____
Total long-term liabilities	$ _____	$ _____	$ _____
Owner's equity:			
Capital stock	$ _____	$ _____	$ _____
Retained earnings	_____	_____	_____
Total owner's equity	$ _____	$ _____	$ _____
Total liabilities & owner's equity	$ _____	$ _____	$ _____

Summary of value:

Assets being purchased (market value) $ _____
Less: liabilities being assumed (market value)   _____

Reasonable price based on assets $ _____

Worksheet 7 continued

Justification of purchase test:

Owner's cash flow from B above $ _____
(includes a salary of $ _____)
Plus:
   Cash to be gained by selling unneeded assets $ _____

   Cash to be gained by trimming inventories   _____
   Cash to be gained by extending payables   _____
   Other cash to be gained   _____
Total cash to be gained $ _____

Less:
   Cash needed to repay debt $ _____
   Cash needed for additional salary   _____
   Cash needed for repairs or replacement   _____
   Cash needed to increase inventories   _____
   Cash needed to increase accounts receivable   _____
   Cash needed to compensate for the
      interest which could have been earned on your down payment   _____
Total cash needed $ _____

Actual cash available (or required) $ _____

First year cash evaluation of purchase

Actual cash available (as above) (A) $ _____
Divided by:
   Cash down payment $ _____
   Plus:
      Additional cash invested or loaned $ _____
      Total cash put into the business (B) $ _____

Cash on cash return (year 1 only) (A) ÷ (B)   _____ %

Worksheet 8
Sources of Money

A. MONEY YOU HAVE

Item Source	On Hand	Available
Cash, stocks, bonds,	$ _____	$ _____
Other investments	_____	_____
Assignable assets	_____	_____
Partnership interests	_____	_____
Personal property	_____	_____
Second job income (annualized)	_____	_____
Spouse income	_____	_____
Insurance policies	_____	_____
Deferred compensation	_____	_____
Retirement accounts	_____	_____
Trusts and annuities	_____	_____
Equity in your home	_____	_____
What you can save (annualized)	_____	_____
Total	_____	_____

B. WHERE YOU CAN BORROW

Source	Specific Contact	Potential Funds Available
Friends and family	_____	$ _____
	_____	_____
Banks or credit union	_____	_____
	_____	_____
Margin/borrowing account insurance policies	_____	_____
	_____	_____
Credit cards	_____	_____
	_____	_____
Asset lenders/factors	_____	_____
	_____	_____
SBA Other federal agencies	_____	_____
	_____	_____
State and local agencies	_____	_____
	_____	_____
Partners	_____	_____
Supplies	_____	_____
Customers	_____	_____
Landlord Insurance companies/foundations	_____	_____
	_____	_____

Worksheet 8 continued

B. WHERE YOU CAN BORROW

Source	Specific Contact	Potential Funds Available
Barter opportunities	$ _____	$ _____
	_____	_____
	_____	_____
Venture capitalists	_____	_____
	_____	_____
Venture groups	_____	_____
	_____	_____
The seller	_____	_____
Total	$ _____	$ _____

5
Starting a Business

The Alternative

Starting a business may sometimes be a better alternative than buying one. It can be cheaper, faster, and less complicated. It can result in a business which matches your criteria exactly.

Some Are Easy to Start

Some businesses, particularly service businesses, are easy to start. Consulting practices, real estate sales companies, repair services, small restaurants, and professional service practices (accounting, legal, financial, medical) can all be started without great difficulty. They may take time to grow and you still may come out ahead by buying, but starting some businesses is easy.

Some Should Be Started

If you have a unique idea or some special personal advantage, you should examine the alternative of starting a business. A special personal advantage might be a patent, a location, or a ready-made client or customer base. You may have a one-of-a-kind source of supply or some special relationships that will ostensibly insure success.

Sometimes It's the Only Way

The business you want may not be available or be affordable. In the case of a unique idea—a new product or service, say—you may have no alternative because there are no such companies.

More often, there are companies which closely match your criteria, but they are either beyond your financial capability or just not for sale.

But the Risk Is Higher

"6 out of every 10 new businesses fail within the first 5 years." This often-quoted statistic shouldn't surprise you. A business which has survived 5 years has proven that its products, prices, location, and its methods of operation are at least acceptable to its market. These key components in the start-up business are all unproven. You may plan to get your first positive cash flow in 12 months, but it may take 24. You may need to have enough cash to keep going for much longer than you thought. You may find that some part of your business is more difficult to maintain than you thought. Perhaps developing new customers takes more selling skills than you possess.

Under-capitalization and lack of required skills are the two major reasons for new business failure. Both are the result of the high uncertainty in business start-ups. A profitable, cash-generating, existing business may cost a premium to buy, but it may have earned it.

The Process

Starting a business involves three things: an idea, a plan, and the resources to carry out the plan.

The Idea

The idea for the new business need not be a new idea or even your idea, but it does have to be a good idea. Here are some questions to pose:

- Does the idea address a real need or want? Is there, or could there be, a demand?
- Will the demand be big enough to support a business? Is the field open or crowded with competition?
- Can the idea actually be transformed into a business? Is the technology available? Will the cost result in a product or service price the market can or will pay?
- Do you have the knowledge and skills required? Has anyone else tried this idea? What was the outcome and why?

Answering these questions takes much thought, a lot of research and, very often, some intuition.

Research is a sometimes maligned activity in new business development. While it's true that research has killed some good ideas, it has killed far more bad ones. Intuition, or gut feel, has launched many a business but not all remained afloat.

Using both research and intuition makes obvious good sense. Even if you have an overwhelming gut feel for your idea, your banker or venture capital firm or, for that matter, your relatives, if they are lending or investing, will want answers to some of the above questions. But it wouldn't matter if no one else asked the questions. You should ask them and do the research to answer them. Why neglect what's available to you? You can always reject the answers in favor of your intuition. In the end, you will have to use intuition to make your judgment on the idea, anyway. Research and analysis can spot extremes and raise warnings, but at best they will provide only estimates and probabilities. You will decide.

The Plan

The plan for a new business will be a paradox. It is based on projections and conjecture. There is no historic pattern or experience base to use as a guide. Yet, the new business plan is expected to be exceedingly detailed. The following paragraphs give a plan outline.

General Concept Statement. Your business idea may not be obvious to anyone else. So, if you expect others to be financial or human resources for you, you will need to provide them with a succinct description. The concept statement should describe the idea and summarize its potential risks and rewards.

The Product or Service. Define your product or service. Show costs for varying levels of production. Try to show the name and the packaging if there is any. Explain any uniqueness or competitive advantage. Describe any protection you have for your product or service. Define the barriers others would face entering the field.

The Market. Define the market in several ways:

Size

Composition or segments

Growth

Location

Demographics

Describe how the buying decision for your product or service is made and who makes it. Present your pricing rationale. Describe the competitive environment. Explain any special features about the market, such as distribution methods, cyclicality, government impact, and so on.

The Organization.   The first organizational issue is the legal form of organization. Table 2.1 contains a description of the various forms and the considerations for selecting one over another. Your attorney and accountant should give you guidance on this choice.

The second organizational issue relates to the structure and the people you plan to have in your new business. Any investor or lender will consider it vital to know how you and your associates are qualified to succeed. Prepare resumes and provide references for yourself and your key people. If you don't have your people in place, describe how and when you will get them.

The Schedule of Events.   Prepare a detailed schedule of all the events that are involved in bringing your new business on stream. The schedule should show *what* the event is; *when* it occurs, including, if it's appropriate, when it begins and ends; and *who* is responsible for each event. No list could be complete, but here is a sample of the kinds of events you should schedule:

- Completing the design of the product or service and completing its packaging
- Selecting suppliers
- Hiring employees
- Choosing a location
- Developing brochures
- Creating advertising and promotion programs
- Obtaining licenses and permits
- Setting up special announcement meetings
- Scheduling customer contacts
- Setting up shop: furniture, telephones, tools, computers, supplies, etc.
- Selecting distributors
- Establishing controls and measurement check points

The Budget. Use the following worksheets to help set up your budget:

- 6A—How much money you need (your personal budget), Chapter 3
- 8—Sources of money (a personal balance sheet and a list of sources of money), Chapter 4
- 9—Business start-up budget format (a more detailed, *monthly* breakdown of income, costs, expenses, and cash flow), at the end of this chapter
- 10—Income statement format (a format for budgeting income and expenses), Chapter 7
- 11—Balance sheet format (a format to project your assets and liabilities), Chapter 7
- 12—Sources and applications of funds format (a format to show the flow of funds in and out of the business), Chapter 7

The new business has two special concerns which the budget must address: cash flow and early warnings of trouble. Worksheet 15 is broken down into monthly detail so you can get a close look at these two key concerns. You should learn quickly what weekly or daily indicators can give even earlier warnings.

Cash flow is doubly important for the new business. Not only do you have to deal with the uncertainty of a start-up business budget, but you have, in all likelihood, had to put your personal and household finances on a matching budget. Make certain you integrate these two budgets to get a complete picture of your cash situation.

Finally, because start-ups have so much uncertainty, you should prepare a contingency budget. The contingency budget should reflect a worst-case situation in which cash flow would be at its reasonably poorest level. Integrating this worst-case contingency budget with your personal budget will point out potential problems and give you the opportunity to make judgments about your plan.

The Resources

The resources to help you start a business include financial resources, physical resources, and information and advice. These resources are not always easy to find or convenient to use. People starting businesses need to be downright ingenious in recognizing and utilizing everything that can help in the extraordinarily difficult task of starting a business.

Financial Resources. In Chapter 4, we presented an array of financing alternatives. Figure 4.2 provides a summary. The sources are relevant for start-ups with one major exception: There is no seller financing. The basic source of money for buying a business is not available to the start-up business.

Physical Resources.   An objective of most start-up businesses is to keep costs low. Physical resources can represent a large part of start-up costs and need special attention. Here are some ideas:

Lease or rent rather than buy. Of course, the lease versus buy decision has to make basic financial sense, but you should be looking for ways to avoid large purchases by renting what you need.

Keep the scale small and avoid extravagances. Investigate used equipment and furniture if you can use it. If you can get by with a small amount of space, find out if there are any "incubator-type" facilities in your area. These are typically facilities sponsored by a development agency or academic institution to aid start-up ventures by providing very small-scale facilities and, often, shared support systems.

Borrow or share where you can. The easiest opportunity for sharing is with office space as covered in Chapter 2. But many others may exist if you have the courage of your convictions to ask for help. People tend to admire the entrepreneur starting a business; they are usually willing to help.

Information and Advice.   This resource is abundant to the point of excess. Figure 7.2 lists 31 sources of information, most of which are applicable to the start-up business. Your start-up doesn't require the intense advice and support of the negotiations and the purchase of a business. But there are a host of details—setting up the books, getting tax identification numbers, obtaining licenses and permits—which will require your advisors' help.

The process of starting a business involves a good idea, a workable plan, and ingenious use of resources.

The Most Important Resource

Your time is the single most important resource in the business start-up. This book tries to make the point that nothing happens in the purchase of a business unless you make it happen. Your time is even more important to the start-up process. There are no employees there to give help, no long-standing bankers, vendors, and suppliers to provide support, and no established customers to offer encouragement.

You have to create and build the enthusiasm that will attract others to your idea and to your business. In the beginning, only you will have your vision and only you will have a stake in its success.

Summary

The alternative of buying a business may be the right one. Some businesses are easy to start and some should be started. Sometimes starting a business is the only way to get going, even though it's more risky.

Worksheet 9
Business Start-Up Budget Format

A. Monthly Profit and Loss Statement

	Month 1	Month 2	Month 3	Month 4	Month 5	Month 6	Month 7	Month 8	Month 9	Month 10	Month 11	Month 12	Total
Sales													
Cost of Sales													
Gross profit													
Expenses:													
Owner's salary													
Owner's benefits and taxes													
No. of people													
Employee salaries													
Employee benefits and taxes													
Rent													
Utilities													
Travel and entertainment													
Selling expenses													
Depreciation													
Insurance													
Supplies													
Interest													
Automobile													
Dues, licenses, subscriptions													
Legal and accounting													
Other													
Other													
Other													
Total Expenses													
Pretax profit													

Worksheet 9 continued

B. Cash Flow Projections

	Month 1	Month 2	Month 3	Month 4	Month 5	Month 6	Month 7	Month 8	Month 9	Month 10	Month 11	Month 12	Total
Cash (opening balance):													
Cash on hand													
Cash in bank													
Near cash investments													
Cash balance beginning													
Cash added:													
Cash sales													
Collections from accounts receivable													
Interest investment income													
Loans to the business													
Other													
Total cash added													
Total Cash Available													
Cash Expenses:													
Purchases of materials & equipment													
Salaries and benefits													
Rent													
Utilities													
Travel and entertainment													
Selling expenses													
Insurance													
Suppliers													
Interest													
Automobile													
Dues, licenses, subscriptions													
Legal and accounting													
Other													
Other													
Other													
Repayment of loan principal													
Taxes													
Total Cash Paid Out													
Cash Balance Ending													
Cash Flow (Deficit) Month													
Cash Flow (Deficit) Cumulative													

6
Finding
the Business

Finding the business, now that you have defined it, involves an orderly process of investigation, contact, and follow through. It takes time, but you will be able to generate a sizable pool of candidates. Figure 6.1 will give you an overview of a business search. A key to success is how well you manage the search process.

Managing the Search

Your search is going to involve contact with a great number of potential sellers, intermediaries, advisors, and others. Because you aren't the only person looking for a business, you will want to establish your credibility. You will want to be recognized as a serious buyer and a business person of substance.

Establish Credibility

You can establish credibility in a direct way by preparing a printed statement of your objectives and criteria and a summary of your qualifications. The objectives and criteria should be specific enough to give the reader a clear idea of what you want but not so detailed or rigorous that they discourage response. Indirect ways to establish credibility involve the use of quality stationery, business cards, and business-like telephone and office procedures. These items were covered in Chapter 2.

Your search needs to be executed crisply and with control. The easi-

Preparation	
Set up to manage the search.	Print copies of your objectives, criteria, and background. Get stationery and business cards. Establish clerical and phone resources.
Develop a list of contact sources.	Consider newspapers, newsletters, trade magazines, business brokers, business owners, lawyers, accountants, bankers, friends, venture capitalists, networks, vendors and suppliers, customers, trade associations, and others.
The active search	
Targeted direct marketing, direct mail, telephone solicitation, and personal contact.	Set objectives, develop key questions for each criterion. Define your targets for each source. Develop lists, select desired format. Develop messages for mail, phone, and personal contact. Execute direct marketing search. Mail the letters, make the phone calls, and knock on the doors. Follow up. Evaluate and develop your pool of candidates.
Advertising (print is suggested).	Decide which of your contact sources can be reached through advertising. Determine how best to reach them. Develop message(s). Place advertising. Follow up. Evaluate and develop your pool of candidates.

Figure 6.1. Diagram of a business search.

est way to stay in control is to organize your activities into manageable segments. Direct mail programs should be large enough to be economic but small enough to permit telephone follow-up. A mailing of 250, with a 5 percent response, would produce 12 to 13 responses. Personal contacts should be staggered far enough apart to allow for reschedules and to allow ample time to pursue any opportunity that might develop.

If you have a computer or your own office services, you can set up planned cycles of contact, follow up, and follow through. If you don't have your own facilities, you can buy the services you need. In almost every city and town you can now find service companies that will type and mail to your mailing list. Most of them can maintain your mailing list and handle responses according to your instructions.

Conducting your search in a business-like manner also means that any contact, correspondence, follow through, or rejection is done with courtesy and professionalism. Your search may take a long while and you should view it as a process of building a network of relationships that you will maintain.

Develop Contacts and Sources

The easiest place to start looking for a business is in the *newspaper*. The common heading used in the classified section is "Business Opportunities." Most of the advertisements will be for small businesses, but occasionally large opportunities will be offered. *The Wall Street Journal,* in its "Mart" section on Wednesdays and Thursdays, contains opportunities of all sizes. *The New York Times* Sunday "Business Opportunities" section runs several pages and contains a very diverse range of opportunities.

Specialized business opportunity newspapers are now being published. Some are national, such as *The Business Opportunity Journal,* and some, such as *The New England Business Opportunity Review,* are regional. (Appendix E lists several business opportunity publications.)

Some banks publish *newsletters* of business opportunities. First National Bank of Maryland and Union Trust Co. in Connecticut are examples. Ask the banks in your area.

Industry trade magazines sometimes contain a classified section with business opportunities. *Restaurant Exchange News,* a regional trade magazine, has extensive offerings. If you have narrowed your search to a particular industry, get copies of industry trade papers and magazines.

Business opportunity ads are usually very cryptic. Only general descriptions are given. Names and location are almost never provided. The reason for such anonymity is to protect the business. Severe harm could be done if customers, employees, suppliers, or competitors knew the business was for sale.

When you answer advertisements, whether by mail or phone, you are trying to do one thing; get information to determine whether the business might meet your criteria. When responding by mail, the approach should be to present yourself as fully qualified as you can so that the advertiser will want to contact you. If you do receive a return contact or if you are answering the ad by phone, you are beginning your active contact, which is discussed later in this chapter.

Your response to an advertisement might be made directly to the seller or to an intermediary, typically a business broker. Your approach to a broker should be the same, but most likely you will be asked some qualifying questions and be asked to meet with the broker to continue the process.

Business brokers offer the next easiest method to explore available business opportunities. Business brokers function much the same as real estate brokers. They are engaged by the business owner and paid a commission to market and sell the business. In that situation the broker is the seller's agent and should be acting in the seller's best interest at all times. It is possible for you to engage the broker under a buyer-broker agreement in which the broker agrees to seek out companies for you. A business broker may have many businesses listed, but few brokers have any cooperative or multiple list arrangements. This means you will need to contact nearly all the business brokers in an area to learn of all the businesses listed with them.

Building good relationships with business brokers should be an early step in your search. Business brokers have an extensive inventory of businesses listed for sale. They have experience that can help you. If you can get brokers to share their listings and their experience with you, you have a valuable resource at no cost. The courtesies you owe the brokers are to deal with them honestly and to remember that their time is the way they earn money.

You can learn the names of business brokers from reading the advertisements or from the yellow pages. You can obtain a list of the brokers who belong to the International Association of Business Brokers by contacting IBBA:

International Business Brokers Association
  POB 704
  Concord, MA 01742
  617-369-5254

You should evaluate business brokers as you would any advisor. Get information on the competence and reputation of anyone whose advice you will be using.

Business owners are excellent contacts for you. Even if their business isn't for sale, they can often tell you who might be selling. They can pass your name along to others. If they ever do decide to sell, your past contact may get you an early look at the business.

Lawyers, accountants, and other personal advisors are sources. They are properly protective of their clients and may be difficult to contact, but they will respond to a professional inquiry if they have a client who may be selling.

Bankers can be helpful in your search. Take the time to meet bankers and find out who handles business accounts. Become known to them. Present your objectives and your background. You may someday be asking the bank to help you finance your purchase so your contact work can be doubly valuable.

Your friends have wide networks of contacts. If you let your friends know your objectives and give them some idea of the kind of company you are seeking, they can be alert for opportunities.

Venture capitalists, merger and acquisition specialists, and *corporate development executives* all live in worlds in which you may find your business. These people may exist independently or inside other companies. Most will be interested in only large transactions. A worthwhile long shot is a call to the corporate development executive or merger and acquisition specialist inside a large company to see if the company may have a small product line or division it wants to sell.

Networks which exist not as part of a club or civic group but solely to be sources of business are a relatively new phenomenon. They were mentioned in Chapter 1 as a basic part of today's entrepreneurship. Some network groups may require that you represent a company, but many are much more informal and hold meetings which are more like mixers. Locating these groups takes some work. Start with your Chamber of Commerce and then check places where such meetings might be held, such as hotels or restaurants. (If no such networks exist in your area, you may want to start one.)

Vendors and suppliers can be good sources of leads. If you know you want to buy a restaurant, find the salespeople for restaurant paper supplies, meat and provisions, equipment, and so on. They have several motives for helping you. Most salespeople pride themselves in knowing what's going on in the market, and that pride is satisfied by displaying the knowledge to you. Salespeople search for ways to help their customers and bringing news of someone looking to buy into their industry might be very helpful. Finally, if you are successful in buying a business in the industry, a salesperson who has helped you will hope that your appreciation will be reflected in purchase orders.

If you do know the exact type of business you want, vendors and suppliers can be a source of contacts that will put you way ahead of others who are looking for similar companies. Not only will you know about companies sooner, but your initiative and determination will be recognized by a seller as signs of your seriousness.

Customers have fewer motives to help you and may be harder to locate, but they still represent a source to find companies for sale.

Industry trade associations are worthwhile contacts for many reasons. They are repositories of membership lists, statistics, and other information about the industry and the people in it. You can learn a great deal about what you are getting into by contacting or possibly joining a trade association for your target industry. Your efforts would have both present and future benefit.

This list of sources is by no means exhaustive. Real estate and stock brokers, civic groups, the Chamber of Commerce, and various state development agencies are just additional sources you might use. The list does prove that there are a great many sources for the determined business seeker. Worksheet 9 can help organize your contacts. Of course just compiling an ingenious list of contact sources won't produce a pool of candidates. You have to actively work these contacts.

Providing Incentives for Leads

Because you are asking people to do something for your economic benefit, you should be willing to compensate them. Compensation for brokers may be regulated in some states, but in almost all of your other contacts you can offer a finder's fee to those who bring you opportunities. You may want to pay the fee only if you actually purchase the business or you may want to encourage leads and be willing to pay if the lead simply meets your criteria. The payment just for providing leads would be relatively small, but the payment for a lead that results in the purchase of a business can be several thousand dollars and be reasonable, depending on the size of the business.

Meaningful incentives will get people to make efforts they would not have made otherwise and will cause them to remember you when they otherwise would have forgotten. Paying people for their time and effort is not only fair, but it is good business. You may want to make your offer to pay quietly or you may want to make it in dramatic style by, say, offering a "$5000 reward" in a newspaper advertisement.

The Active Search

Once you have provided for your clerical and administrative needs and have generated an extensive stock of contacts, you can devise your active search program (see Figure 6.1). It's the active search program that will lead you to businesses before other buyers find them. You will be able to find businesses that owners haven't actively tried to sell but which are available if an offer is made. Your active inquiry may be the event that initiates an owner's interest in selling.

Your program should use targeted direct marketing techniques and well planned advertising.

Targeted Direct Marketing

Targeted direct marketing, as the name implies, involves your direct solicitation to specific contacts. *Direct mail* is the easiest and broadest reaching of the direct marketing techniques. *Telephone solicitation* is an effective method for a smaller and more qualified list of contacts. *Personal contact* and canvassing is the most powerful but most time consuming direct marketing activity. The three techniques are most often combined to achieve maximum effectiveness. The steps involved in targeted direct marketing are:

Setting objectives

Defining the target

Developing lists

Creating the message

Executing the search

Following up and evaluating results

Setting Objectives

The objectives you establish for your direct marketing contacts will depend on the type of contact.

Objectives with Advisors and Others. With accountants, attorneys, vendors, trade associations, friends, and other business people who are indirectly involved, your primary objective is to learn the name of a company which may be for sale. If you can get an introduction, that's a big plus. Another objective is to use the occasion of the contact to network to others who may be helpful. The question, "Do you know anyone who...," is a good network builder. A third objective is to leave a clear, positive impression with the contact so that he or she will remember to call you when a company meeting your general criteria does become available.

Objectives with Intermediaries. The objective for direct contact with brokers and other intermediaries is different. You try to build a more substantive relationship. It was mentioned earlier that they can be a major resource in your efforts to buy a business. You want to convince the intermediaries that you are a serious, qualified buyer who will act quickly and professionally when they present opportunities which meet your criteria.

Objectives with Targeted Business Owners. There are special objectives for your direct contacts with owners of businesses who might be candidates for your pool of opportunities. The overriding objective is to determine whether the company is for you and whether it is, or could be, for sale. View your efforts with these business owners as a series of contacts. Owners are cautious when answering questions about their business. You will need to earn their confidence. Earlier in this chapter we presented ways to help establish credibility (written objectives, a personal summary, business cards, etc.). Use these tools in a well-organized, professional way in your contacts with business owners. An objective for any contact you make should be to learn as much as you can about the industry and the companies in it.

Defining Your Target

The key to success in direct marketing is the quality of your list, and the key to the quality of your list is how well you define your target. Defining some of your targets is easy. All accountants in your geographic area are target contacts. The same may be true for attorneys, bankers, and brokers.

Some contacts may need to be defined more narrowly. Using our previous example of vendors as contacts to learn about restaurants, you would need to identify the vendor type (i.e., paper supplier) and the industry being served (restaurants). Consultants, venture capitalists, customers, and trade associations all need this kind of refinement to be worthwhile contacts.

Defining the companies you want to contact is not so simple. This most important category of target contacts needs the most careful definition. Fortunately you have already defined the kinds of companies you want to target. (In Chapter 3 you established explicit criteria for the company you want. In Chapter 4 you developed a working approximation of what you can afford.) The better job you do to refine your list, the better the results of your search.

Developing Your List

The next step in your active search is to convert these now defined contact targets into real names, addresses, and phone numbers. You need to develop your list.

Working with lists has become an easier task now that computers are commonplace. There are several types of software which permit easy construction of a database of the names on your list. Word processing software to generate letters, envelopes, and labels is commonplace. There are service companies that can perform all of these tasks, usually on a per-name price basis.

Buying Lists.   The easiest way to develop a list is to buy one. List companies and brokers can supply you with lists of all the target contacts we have used as examples. Some lists can be refined to your specifications. The cost and quality of lists varies greatly. Prices range from $20 per thousand names to several hundred dollars per thousand. Some lists are well maintained and accurate while others are not. The list provider should advise you of the "percent deliverable" for any list you buy. A good source of help in locating and dealing with list companies is an advertising agency which is active in the direct mail field. Appendix E provides the names of several list companies.

Compiling Lists.   You may prefer to compile your own list. Getting the names, addresses, and phone numbers of most of your contacts is as simple as looking in the yellow pages or buying a membership directory. Your network of friends and personal contacts is probably already compiled into a list.

The list of target companies will take some effort to compile but not as much as you might think. There are directories for almost every industry segment imaginable. There are even directories of directories (see Appendix E). These directories can often help you key in on such specific criteria as size, location, number of employees, and years in business. Some may even provide the names of the owners or chief executives.

Directories can be expensive to buy. Here are some suggested sources that may permit you to use their directories.

- College libraries
- Chambers of Commerce
- Trade associations
- Advertising agencies

- Marketing departments of companies which sell to your target companies

In addition, there are full directory services which operate across all industries. Two of the most well known are Dun and Bradstreet and Thomas Publishing Company, publishers of *Thomas' Register.* Dun's Marketing Services, a Dun and Bradstreet division, provides standard or customized directory listings and will produce the mailing labels if you order them.

Getting lists of businesses, then, can be as commonplace as looking in the yellow pages or as obscure as getting the attendance list from a conference your targets would have attended.

The Format for Your List. The last thing you need to know about ordering lists is that you must specify the format you want. Lists come on magnetic (computer) tape, pressure sensitive (peel-and-stick) labels, and Cheshire (machine-applied) labels. You would want the magnetic tape if you were working with a service firm which uses it. Cheshire labels are usually cheaper but require a printer or mailer to apply them, sometimes at an extra cost. They are not economical for short runs. Pressure sensitive labels cost more but are easy to apply. If you are doing the mailing yourself, this is the format to order.

If you are compiling your own lists and using a personal computer, you can buy one of several software products which will manage your list and the printing of labels or envelopes.

Creating Your Message

Once you have a well-defined and usable list of contacts, you can turn to the second most important element in your direct marketing program: the message you send. The purpose of your message is to get a response. Whether you are using mail, the telephone, or personal canvassing, you will need to send enough in your message to trigger the desired response from the desired target.

Messages for Direct Mail. Some sample letters for the mail segment of your direct marketing program are shown in Figures 6.2, 6.3, and 6.4.

Messages for Telephone Solicitation. Making "cold" telephone calls can be a stomach-churning experience for some people. The prospect of personal rejection is both unappealing and probable. There are two things that can help you overcome the apprehension you may have. One is simply experience. People who were frightened to call strangers

Mr. James Stevens, Esq.
Stevens and Jones Attorneys
37 Arch Street St.
Petersburg, Florida 33705

Dear Attorney Stevens:

I am interested in buying a business in the Tampa/St. Petersburg area.

I would especially like to find a lumberyard or building supply center where my 20 years of building products experience would be applicable. Garden centers, landscaping companies, and specialty contractors, such as those who install swimming pools or tennis courts, would also be of interest.

I have substantial cash on hand and an excellent credit standing. Bank references are available. I will move quickly and professionally to evaluate any candidate you may bring forward.

If you would like to know more about me and my objectives please write or call.

OR

I will take the liberty of calling you to explain my objectives and to learn whether you have any clients who might be candidates.

Thank you for your consideration.

Yours truly,

Christopher Cronin
Telephone (813) 555-1641

Figure 6.2. Sample letter for advisors.

learn through experience that success can be achieved and failure is anonymous.

The other key to helping you with cold calls is the use of a prepared opening script. Experts in the field of telemarketing advise lots of rehearsal, which will instill confidence and make you more comfortable and natural with your presentation. The scripts for contacting accountants, attorneys, brokers, trade associations, vendors, and other nonowners are paraphrases of the direct mail letters. The scripts for owners requires one major revision. Unless the owner answers the phone, you may have trouble getting through to talk with the owner. Here are some approaches which assume you do not have the advantage of the owner's name:

"Hello, my name is Chris Cronin. Who am I talking with, please?"

("This is Bob.")

Ms. Stephanie Davis
Membership Director
Florida Building Products Association
211 Main Street
Tampa, FL 33615

Dear Ms. Davis:

I am interested in buying a lumberyard or building supply center in the Tampa/St. Petersburg area. Garden centers, landscaping companies, and specialty contractors would also be of interest.

I have over 20 years experience in the industry and I am prepared to move quickly and professionally on any opportunity. I have substantial cash on hand and an excellent credit standing.

Because you are a key part of the industry, I would especially appreciate any help and advice you could give me. Please be assured that I will comply with any requirements for confidentiality or anonymity you may suggest.

I will take the liberty of calling you to more fully explain my objectives and to ask your advice on how to proceed.

Thank you in advance for your consideration.

Yours truly,

Christopher Cronin
Telephone (813) 555-1641

Figure 6.3. Sample letter for vendors, customers, trade associations, etc.

"I'm trying to locate the owner of Steck's Lumberyard. Are you the owner?"

(If 'yes,' use the letter to owners as a script. If 'no,' continue.)

"Oh. May I ask who the owner is?"

(If you get the name, ask to speak to him or her. If you are asked to give your reason for wanting to know, continue.)

"Bob, I'm interested in buying a lumberyard in this area and I thought the owner of Steck's might know if any are for sale. I'm sure the owner would be interested in hearing about my plans."

(If you are still refused the name, continue.)

"Say, I can understand the owner's desire to keep a low profile. But, would you do this please, Bob? Would you give the owner my name and phone number and explain that I am looking to buy a lumberyard and I would really appreciate some advice. The name is Chris

Mr. Fred Steck
Steck's Lumber
11277 Bayside
St. Petersburg, FL 33705

Dear Mr. Steck:

I am interested in buying a lumberyard in the Tampa/St. Petersburg area. Although I have not heard that your business is for sale, I decided to approach you directly in the event that you may have a desire to sell.

I have over 20 years experience in lumber and building products. My financial situation is solid and I have cash available.

If your business isn't for sale, perhaps you could forward this letter to another business owner who may be interested in selling. Garden centers, landscaping companies, and specialty contractors would also be of interest to me.

If you would like to know more about me and my objectives, please write or call.

OR

I will take the liberty of calling you to explain more fully my objectives and to learn whether you or someone you know may have an interest in selling. Thank you for your consideration.

Yours truly,

Christopher Cronin
Telephone (813) 555-1641

Figure 6.4. Sample letter for company owners.

Cronin and the number is (813) 555-1641. Thanks for your help, Bob."

(Optional)

"I'd like to call you later to find out the owner's reaction. Thank you. Goodbye."

Other variations are required when you are told the owner is out or unavailable. Emphasize to the person you are talking with that it is important to the owner to know that a potential lumberyard buyer is seeking advice. When you do get a business owner on the phone, the questions presented in Figure 6.5 can get you started.

Messages for Personal Contact. Personal contact and canvassing is the most time-consuming direct marketing technique, but it is also the most powerful. Personal contact allows you to make a stronger impression.

Whether you are contacting business owners by telephone or in person, you will need some special techniques to get information from these cautious people.

Getting permission to ask questions is the first step. Phrases such as "May I ask..." or "Would you allow me..." help lower the owners' concern by giving them control over the conversation. Another device to gain permission is to ask "How would I find out..." or "How would you suggest that I...."

Having good questions to ask is the second step. You have your criteria, including some financial parameters, already established.

You can convert these criteria into specific opening questions you can ask, either over the telephone or during personal contact, to see if this business might satisfy them.

CRITERIA	OPENING QUESTIONS
Content of the business	Could you please describe your business—what it does, who its customers are, and how it earns income?
People intensity	What's the composition of your work force?
Status and image/working conditions	How do you spend your time in the business?
Growth potential	How old is the business? How long have you owned it? How would you describe the growth of the business?
Basic financial	Can you share with me your recent sales performance? Are you profitable?
Location	Where are you located? How did you come to be located there?
Basic financial (real estate)	How much space do you use? Do you own or rent?
Competition	How would you describe your competition? Who are some typical competitors?
Risk	What do you see as the biggest risks in a business like yours?
Basic financial	(If you know the business is for sale) What are you asking for the business?

Figure 6.5. Obtaining information from business owners.

Your personal presence emphasizes your determination. Being face to face allows you to do a better job establishing rapport and getting information.

Prepare for personal contact by typing or printing copies of your objectives and background summary. Business cards are a must. The message for personal contact is a variation of your direct mail letter. If you are making cold canvassing calls on businesses, the telephone script and the questions presented in Figure 6.5 are both relevant.

If your personal contact is a follow up to your mail and telephone work or if you have otherwise made appointments for your personal contact, you are set to conduct this part of your active search. If you plan to do cold calls, that is, calls without an appointment, plan on doing a lot of call backs to contact the people who will not or cannot meet with you when you make your call. Your call back can be another personal visit or a contact by mail or phone. If you cannot make the personal contact, do the next best thing and try to get your printed material to the targeted contact.

The targeted direct marketing portion of your active search is now ready to go. You have your list of contacts, your messages, and their style of presentation.

Advertising

The advertising portion of your active search is based on reaching the right people with the right message so that they will contact you.

The Right People

The right people to target with advertising are business owners, business brokers, and other intermediaries. It is unlikely that any of the other contacts we have discussed would take action on your advertisement.

The Right Method

Having decided who the right people are, you need to decide the best method of reaching them. While other media may be interesting to consider, we are going to assume that print advertising is the best method for reaching our targets.

Newspapers are the best print medium to reach brokers and intermediaries, who regularly read the "Business Opportunities" section of newspapers. Which newspapers you use will depend on the business you are seeking. If you are looking for a small or locally oriented business, the local newspaper may be all you need. If the business is large or specialized, you may want to add *The Wall Street Journal* or one of the specialized business opportunity newspapers (See Appendix E). Newspaper classified advertising will reach business owners who read the business opportunities, but those are a small percentage of the owners you want to reach.

Deciding where to advertise to reach business owners takes some analysis of what they read. Trade papers and magazines are good prospects. If the business has a special focus such as sports, you may want to use that section of your local newspaper.

If the business you want has no trade publications or special focus, accept the fact that any advertising will be useful only with intermediaries. After you select the publications you are going to use, call to find out the procedures and rates for advertising.

The Right Message

The next step is to write the advertisement based on the rate information you obtained and the message you want to send. The objective of your ad is to get a response from your target. If you put yourself in the target's shoes, you can pretty much determine what would trigger that response:

You are a potential buyer.

You are qualified.

You have money.

Here are two sample ads of average length. The first assumes you have a specific kind of company in mind.

WANTED TO BUY
LUMBERYARD/BUILDING CENTER

20-year industry exec seeks lumberyard, building, or garden center or similar business in Tampa/St. Petersburg. Cash available. Will structure deal to meet seller's objectives. Replies held confidential. C. Cronin (813) 555-1641

Any lumberyard owner or business broker would understand that ad and would respond if appropriate.

Here is an ad to use when you don't know exactly what you want for a business:

Business exec with $200,000 cash plus strong credit seeks distribution or manufacturing company in Tampa/St. Petersburg. Will structure deal to meet seller's objectives. Replies held confidential. C. Cronin (813) 555-1641

Note that in the first ad, no mention was made of the amount of cash available, but in the second ad the amount was declared. In the first ad, you have such a narrow target you want to get every and any lumber-yard opportunity. In the second ad, your specifications are so broad you need to put some kind of filter in the ad. The ad presumes you don't care how small the business is, but there is some upper limit.

You may want to run your ad several times. Owners might need to see the ad a few times to let the idea of selling develop into the action of calling you. Every response generated by your search activities needs to be evaluated and followed through. If a lead or candidate is generated which is outside your criteria, thank the source and encourage more appropriate leads.

A Disadvantage of the Active Search

The active search does have one disadvantage when compared to reading ads or talking with brokers. The active search will bring you in contact with business owners who may not want to sell but who are curious about what their business is worth. The expression you might hear is "every business is for sale if the price is high enough." You can waste lots of time with these owners unless you quickly determine whether they are potential sellers. Ask straight out what the price is and say that, in order to know whether that price is fair, you need to see the financial records. If you are asked to offer a price, point out that you are more than willing to make an offer but you will, of course, need to see the financial records to be able to work up a price that is fair. If the owner refuses to let you see the books, you can either ask him or her for an alternative way to proceed or you can assume the seller is not serious and move on to another business.

Follow Up and Evaluation

Follow up on every lead you get from the active search and your advertising. Even if the lead is a poor one, it may be a connection to one that is worthwhile. Another reason for following up on all leads is to reinforce your reputation as a competent business person.

Evaluate your leads by comparing them to your criteria. If the lead or candidate is within your criteria, set up an information file and a schedule of contacts. A Company Profile Data Form to help you organize key information about each company you are entering in your pool is in Appendix F.

Summary

You are now able to generate your pool of candidate companies. You know how to identify sources and contacts. You know how to develop lists of contact names and how to implement an active search. You know how to use direct marketing techniques and advertising to get the response you want. Worksheet 10 and Figure 6.1 will help you organize your search.

Worksheet 10
Sources and Contacts for Locating Businesses

Source	Specific Contact/Comments
Newspapers	_____
Newsletters	_____
Trade magazines	_____
Business brokers	_____
Business owners	_____
Other business people	_____
Lawyers, accountants, other advisors	_____
Bankers/investment bankers	_____
Friends	_____
Venture capitalists, merger and acquisition specialists, corporate development executives	_____
Networks	_____
Vendors and suppliers	_____
Customers	_____
Industry trade associations	_____
Others	_____

7
Analyzing the Business

When your pool of candidates produces a company that seems to meet your criteria, you begin the work of analyzing your business. During this phase, you will be relying increasingly on your advisors.

Managing Your Advisors

The three advisors most involved are accountants, attorneys, and intermediaries. If there is an intermediary, you need to be certain of his or her loyalty and responsibility. Most work for the seller. Get a clear definition of his or her function.

Intermediaries

Some intermediaries have full power to negotiate while others are only communication conduits. Some are active and creative in structuring deals and some only transmit offers. Levels of skill and experience vary. Ask how he or she operates. Find out how the seller wants the process to go. Intermediaries are paid to complete transactions and are normally very helpful to the process. However, you cannot rely solely on the seller's agent for your information and advice. You need to manage the intermediary as a part of managing this final phase of the process.

Accountants

Managing your accountant begins with the kind of arrangement you have with him or her. By this time, your accountant should be well aware of your objectives and your resources.

Unless you are secure with your own skills, you will want your accountant to perform tests and analyses and provide you with recommendations. The two of you should discuss the limitations of using accounting statement and tax return information and the risks of using adjusted information such as will most often be used in analyzing small businesses. Both kinds of information are needed and the two of you have to agree on how best to use them. You may want your accountant to advise you on how to structure your transaction. Whatever you want from your accountant should be made clear between you, and, if you don't already know, ask your accountant how you will be charged.

You should know, too, that accountants can face a special dilemma when advising on the purchase of a business. If a buyer relies heavily on an accountant and buys a business on which the accountant has favorably advised and then has trouble (even of the buyer's own making), he or she might be the kind of buyer to hold the accountant liable. If, on the other hand, the client buys a business which the accountant has advised against and the business is successful, the accountant has only to be happy for the client's success. Therefore, there may be pressure on the accountant to avoid positive recommendations. You can help avoid that pressure by letting your accountant know you are going to welcome advice from your advisors to make the final decision, but you will accept responsibility for your own judgment.

Attorneys

Managing your attorney involves much of the same discipline. Have a discussion about how you will work together. You may want your attorney to just review the contract and closing documents or you may want him or her to completely handle the negotiations. In between these extremes is advice and counsel on the purchase transaction. If you have already selected the company you are going after, your attorney might be able to estimate the complexity of the transaction and thereby the time and charges you might budget.

Your Team

The last step in managing your accountant and your attorney is to develop them into your team. Their work is interrelated. How this purchase will affect your total tax situation requires their coordination. Estate planning is another area of common interest. These two advisors may be excellent resources in your negotiating tactics. You want your objective—buying a business—to become their objective. With your team in place, you can begin your evaluation.

Evaluating the Business

Gathering information and analyzing all the factors surrounding the business can seem like an overwhelming task. Just remember at all times that you do *not* have to buy *this* business. Most assuredly, you don't have to buy it in a hurry. While you should conduct your analysis with consideration for the time of others, that does not mean you should be rushed.

You have your accountant and attorney as advisors and you can hire specialized advisors if you need them. Yet, with all this help, you will make any final decision on imperfect and incomplete information because there is no other. Buying a business is a risk. The challenge is to minimize the risk as best you can.

One constraint in your evaluation activities is the need for confidentiality. We mentioned in Chapter 4 that the concern for confidentiality by the seller is genuine. It should be your concern, too. If knowledge of the potential sale of the business upsets customers, employees, the landlord, or others, you may be the one who suffers. Telling a friend or neighbor about your plan may get it spread to the entire community. This requirement for confidentiality means extra care should be taken when gathering information.

We can break this complex task of evaluation into steps. First, we'll decide *what* information we need to have. Then comes a list of all the sources *where* the information might be found. Finally, we'll work on *how* to analyze the information you uncover.

The Information Needed

You need and want considerable information about the company and its environment (see Figure 7.1). You also need one piece of information about the owner. Try to find out the reason the owner is selling. It can be an important clue to the condition of the business. Unfortunately, you may get acceptable sounding answers such as "other business interests" or "retirement" when the real reason is "I can't hire any help" or "competition is killing me." You need to probe any reason you are given. Ask to know more about the other business interests or the retirement. If you ask in several ways about the owner's future plans, you may get some insights.

The basic plan to obtain company information is merely to follow

The owner's reason for selling
Company history
The company's purpose, what it does
People
Organization
Facilities
Equipment
Technology
Market
Competition
Company operations:
  Manufacturing
  Legal
  Marketing and sales
  Accounting and finance
General strengths and weaknesses
Outside factors
Financial performance
Financial projections (Some buyers and intermediaries actually base
their analysis and pricing on projections rather than history. They
believe the future results of the business are more indicative of the
business' value to the buyer.)

Figure 7.1. What information is needed?

down a list of business factors and ask questions. The opening questions
are designed to get you into the topic. Your direction after that will be
governed by the answers you get and the importance of the factor to
this particular company. Here are some opening questions:

Business factor	Opening questions
History	When and how did the company start? What has been its history of ownership and activity? Who owns the company now and in what form is the ownership?
Purpose	What is the fundamental nature of the business? What does it do? Why does it exist? Does it have a plan or direction?
People	Who are they? How many are there? How long have they been there? What do they do? Are they competent? Are they satisfied? Are any of them critical to success? Is there a union? How well are they paid? Are there enough of them? Is there a manager other than the owner? Will key people leave if a sale takes place?

(Continued)

Business factor	Opening questions
Organization	What is it? Does it work well? What function does the owner play? Are there organizational policies and practices? Is there depth in the organization?
Facilities (plant or office)	What are they? Is the size right? Own or rent? What are the terms and length of the lease? Can it be assumed? Is the facility where it should be? What is the condition of the facility? What would it take to relocate?
Equipment	What is it? Is it modern? Well kept? What is the percent of use? Is there enough or not enough? Who supplies it? Who maintains it? Could it be easily sold?
Technology	Are company methods and techniques modern? Are products and services modern? How does the company provide for innovation? Does technology change rapidly? What computer systems does the company use?
Market	What or who is the company's market? How large is it? Is it growing or declining? Does it have many or few customers? Is it style or fad based?
Competition	Who are the competitors? Is competition increasing? Do competitors have any special advantages? Who has what share of the market and how is that changing? Are any competitors for sale?
Manufacturing	What is the manufacturing process? What is the total capacity? How much is available? What would it cost to expand? How is productivity measured? Any special skills required? Any special dependence on suppliers? Any problems with EPA or labor?
Legal	Is the company involved in litigation? Is there some exposure? What contracts or obligations does the company have? Who is the company's attorney? Does the company require licenses to operate or is it otherwise regulated? Does it have any patents? To what associations does the company belong? Does the company have adequate insurance?
Marketing and sales	What are the key marketing activities and techniques? How many people do what tasks? How are the products and services perceived in the marketplace? What have been the trends in sales volume and prices? How are prices set? How are salespeople hired, trained, and compensated? How many customers does the company have? Are sales concentrated among a few customers? How geographically spread are the customers? Has the company lost any customers? Are customers long established? Do they sign contracts? Will they stay on after the sale?

(Continued)

Business factor	Opening questions
Accounting and finance	How is the accounting and/or financial function organized? Is it adequate for the company's needs? Are systems and reports satisfactory? Who is the company's outside accountant? Who is the company's banker? Are adequate lines of credit established? Does the company pay its bills on a schedule?
General	What are the strengths and weaknesses of the company? What area needs the most immediate improvement? Where does the company's greatest potential lie? What is the biggest threat to the company?
Outside factors	Are there any special problems or opportunities relating to general economic conditions, world trade, governmental agencies, or other outside factors?
Financial Performance (Before asking the questions, determine if the information you have is complete and accurate. Get 3 to 5 years of figures if you can.)	Is the company profitable? How profitable? Is it growing? Is enough cash being generated to operate the business? What adjustments are needed to get from the accountant's profit to the owner's cash flow? Study trends.
Balance sheet	What has been the trend of inventory? How much is finished goods, how much is raw material, how much is work in progress? Is the inventory worth the value? Has the level of accounts receivable varied? How old are they? Are they owed by a few or many customers? What are the fixed and other assets? How have fixed assets been valued and depreciated? What market value do they have? Has the level of accounts payable varied? To whom are they owed? Are they current? Identify the debt and each creditor. How much is it? What is the trend? How old is it?
Income (P&L) statement	What have been the trends in sales? In costs? Have any expense items changed significantly? Is adequate money being spent on repairs (or any other item)?
Ratios	If you can, set up the following ratios/percentages: return on investment, return on sales, individual expense items to sales, costs to sales, current assets to current liabilities, income (cash) to debt payments, receivable turns per year, inventory turns per year, salaries and benefits as a percent of total expenses. (There will be further discussion on ratios later in the chapter.)

Many more questions can, and will, be generated as you actually dig out the information. Finding the information is our next task.

The Information Sources

The seller and the intermediary will be your primary sources of information, but you do not have to rely on these sources alone. Figure 7.2 is a list of 31 different sources of information. Not all will be relevant to your company, but you may find some surprisingly good sources in the list. You can locate all but a few of these sources on your own. The rest you can reach or use by working with your advisors. Hard detective work on those sources should yield the information you are seeking (and more). Now that you have it, you need to decide what the information means.

Analyzing the Information

You are first faced with the task of sorting through all the data you have gathered and organizing it. There is a Company Profile Data Form in Appendix F to help you organize and record your information. It also helps you match the facts about a company to the requirements you established earlier, requirements such as risk and your criteria for buying a business. Part of the Company Profile Data Form will be shown as

The seller	Tax returns
Company records	Franchise records
Associations	Employees (and former
Competitors	employees)
Consultants	Banks
Suppliers	Government records
Seller's advisors	Your advisors
Newspapers and magazines	Library
Neighboring businesses	Your networks
Chamber of Commerce	Better Business Bureau
Court/land records	Landlord
Unions	Bonding company
Patent office	Credit reporting companies
Insurance policies and agents	Stockbroker
Real estate broker	Private investigator
The intermediary	Your own personal observation

Figure 7.2. Sources of information.

Worksheet 11 at the end of this chapter. The qualitative process of analysis you will use is called forced rating. It is simply a 1 to 10 or 1 to 6 scale that causes you to explicitly rate your findings. The quantitative portion of the process will be conventional financial analysis.

Qualitative Analysis

You gathered information in some or all of 17 business factors. As a summary and reminder, here they are: history, purpose, people, organization, facilities, equipment, technology, market(s), competition, manufacturing, legal, marketing and sales, accounting and finance, general, outside factors, reason for selling, and financial performance. In Worksheet 11, rate the combined weight of your evaluation of these factors against each of your criterion and risk elements. The rating process does two things:

- It forms an integrated idea of desirability.

- It points out extremes and suggests areas for further investigation.

The rating is imperfect because it assumes an equal value for each criterion and for each risk factor. Nonetheless, you have followed a logical path to this point at which you can make your first judgments about whether this business is for you. If the business is far outside your preferred degree of risk or does not at all satisfy your criteria, there is no need to analyze the quantitative data. If your judgment does not eliminate the candidate, you move to the numbers.

Quantitative Analysis

What follows is an overview of fairly conventional financial analyses. The degree of your own skills in this area and the complexity of the data will dictate the extent you involve your accountant.

Comparative Analysis.   One kind of quantitative analysis involves comparison. Facts, figures, and ratios developed for the business you are considering are compared with standards of some kind. The most readily available standards are the company's previous financial statements. Comparing current and historic financial performance is a sure way to spot significant deviations in current performance. Comparisons can also use more or less generally accepted benchmarks such as a 2 to 1 ratio between current assets and current liabilities. Your accountant or banker can provide you with these interesting but very imprecise rules of thumb.

Other comparisons can be made with industry norms. Basic financial figures and ratios are available for many kinds and sizes of business. Industry trade associations may publish them. Trade papers and magazines sometimes publish an annual edition of financial performance ratios. Your stockbroker has access to performance statistics for many kinds of businesses. The government offers industry financial statistics through the SBA and the Department of Commerce. Two comprehensive sources of ratios are *The Almanac of Business and Industrial Ratios* and *Financial Studies of the Small Business.* *

Financial Statement Analysis. A second kind of quantitative analysis involves the interpretation of the financial statement contents. Here we are not trying to compare but rather to understand and evaluate.

Both kinds of quantitative analyses, *comparison* and *financial statement analysis,* are based on ratios, turnover rates, return rates, percentage analyses, sensitivity analyses, breakeven analyses and an analysis of the sources and application of funds (cash).

Ratio Analysis. Ratio analysis is a common quantitative technique. The relationship between two financial statement items can be reduced to a simple standardized ratio which is easy to compare and understand. Here are some common ratios and their implications:

- *Current ratio.* This is the ratio of current assets to current liabilities. It's an indicator of a company's ability to meet its short-term obligations. It is an indicator of liquid strength, at least in the short term.

- *The acid test ratio.* An even more stringent liquidity measure. It, too, uses the ratio between current assets and current liabilities, but inventory and other nonliquid assets are removed from the current asset category.

- *Fixed assets to long-term liabilities.* Although this is not a much used test in small businesses, it does show the degree of security behind the long-term debt.

- *Turnover.* The two common turnover ratios are inventory and accounts receivable. They are good comparative measures to help you

---

*Troy, Leo: *Almanac of Business and Industrial Financial Ratios,* Prentice-Hall, Englewood Cliffs, NJ. *Financial Studies of the Small Business,* Financial Research Associates, Winter Haven, FL.

analyze how well your candidate company does in managing these two asset investments. Inventory turnover is typically calculated by dividing the cost of goods by the average inventory. (Year beginning inventory plus year ending inventory divided by 2.) Accounts receivable turnover is determined by dividing net sales by average receivables. (Year beginning receivables plus year end receivables divided by 2.)

■ *Return on investment.* In this book, we compute return on investment using the adjusted owner's cash flow as the return figure and the net market value of our investment as the investment figure. We use these measures because they produce information useful in making an investment decision. However, to be able to compare your candidate company to conventional standards of return on investment, you will need to use conventional measures. The conventional measures do vary from industry to industry and it is vital that you understand them. Return on investment in industries with large capital investments will bear no comparison to returns in certain service industries. For example, when analyzing residential real estate companies, return on investment is a secondary measure. The analyses are more often expressed in terms of percent of net revenue (company dollar). Just determine how your standard is derived and use the same method of calculation.

Return percentages are a critical part of your analysis because they reduce all of the financial data to one key number. Because of the apparent precision employed in computing the return percentage, there is a tendency to misuse it. It is a good comparative measure (if your standard of comparison is valid) but not a good evaluative measure. The percent return on investment is not a measure of return on your *actual cash* investment unless you invest all cash.

Return on investment (ROI) has one other practical shortcoming in that it does not measure any appreciation the investment may have enjoyed. The following real estate investment example can demonstrate these shortcomings (ignore any tax implications).

If you bought a small shopping center for $1 million and received income after all expenses of $25,000, you would have a gross ROI of 2½ percent. But if you only put $100,000 in cash as a down payment, you could view your cash-on-cash ROI as 25 percent.

Let's further assume you sell the shopping center after a year for $1,100,000. Does that $100,000 profit represent a 10 percent return on the $1 million or does it represent a 100 percent return on the $100,000 cash you actually invested? In fact, it means both things. Remember that the actual amount of $100,000 is the same; only your definition of "in-

vestment" (the degree of financing) changed. Be aware of two principles that apply to this part of your analysis:

1. A high level of financing can make a bad business affordable, but it
   doesn't make it a good business.
2. The basic rule of financing says you borrow only if you can earn
   more than it costs you to borrow.

If you put down very little cash and borrow a great deal, you may end
up using all your income for debt repayments.

Your very important analysis of return on investment needs to involve not only the historic financial statement rates of return but your
projections of returns based on your own financing plan.

Cost and Expense Analysis.   This form of analysis can be very enlight-
ening because it allows you to compare your target company with others, with its own history, and with your own judgment. The analysis is
done by dividing sales by the individual cost and expense items. Here is
a simplified example:

Item	Amount	Percent of Sales
Sales	$700,000	100
Cost of goods	315,000	45
Gross profit	$385,000	55
Salaries	84,000	12
Rent	35,000	5
Utilities	14,000	2
Interest	21,000	3
Selling expenses	35,000	5
Administration	42,000	6
Transportation	14,000	2
Total expenses	$245,000	35
Pretax profit	$140,000	20

Be alert for changes in trends and numbers which seem outside the normal standards and outside your common sense idea of what is normal.

Sensitivity Analysis.   As the name suggests, this quantitative analysis
attempts to determine how sensitive the company's performance is to

changes in income, costs, and expenses. The analysis is accomplished by posing "what if" questions:

What if the rent doubles?

What if I add two people?

What if sales go up or go down 5 percent?

What if I raise prices 10 percent and lose 1 percent in volume?

Your objective is to get a feel for where the business is most vulnerable and where it has the most potential.

Break-Even Analysis. This is a special form of sensitivity analysis that allows you to better understand the relationships among sales, fixed costs, variable costs, and profit. It assumes that some costs such as rent, administration, and insurance are more or less fixed in the short term, while others such as the cost of materials and selling commissions vary with volume. After deciding whether the cost or expense is fixed or variable, you construct a chart similar to the one in Figure 7.3.

This is a particularly useful analysis to test or verify a seller's claims. For example, if a seller claims that all a business needs is a little attention to sales when, in fact, the problem is high fixed overhead, this type of analysis can be very revealing. It will show just how much of an increase in sales is needed to improve profitability.

Sources and Application of Funds. This analysis will show you, for a specific period of time, whether the company you are considering consumed more or less cash than it generated. The analysis uses a comparison between the balance sheets of two periods and information from the income (P&L) statement.

The income statement has two items which affect the analysis: profit (or loss) and noncash expenditures such as depreciation. Profit and depreciation are sources of funds.

The simple rules to follow with the balance sheet are:

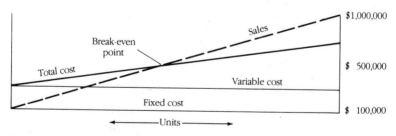

Figure 7.3. Break-even analysis.

An increase in assets is a use of funds.

A decrease in assets is a source of funds.

An increase in liabilities is a source of funds.

A decrease in liabilities is a use of funds.

If the company you are considering has professionally prepared statements, they will normally include a statement of sources and application of funds.

Help to Analyze the Information

You have several sources of help in analyzing the information you have gathered. We have mentioned your advisors, industry statistics and standards, and company history. Real estate appraisers, inventory appraisal companies, specialized equipment appraisers, and dealers are others who can help.

The Seller's Advisors

You can also use the seller and the seller's advisors. No one knows more about the business than they. Often there is no other way to understand some fact or figure but to ask the seller. Some sellers are candid to the point of total disclosure. The obvious risk in asking these sources is they are selling and want to present the best picture possible. The offset against that risk is the fact that the seller is probably going to finance your purchase. The seller knows if you discover you have been deceived, you are going to be less than cooperative in repaying your debt. Do as you would with any advice and evaluate the source as well as the information.

One source of help may take some selling on your part but is worth the effort. The seller's banker will know more about the business than almost anyone. If you have the choice of selecting the seller's banker to be your banker, your motive to work with this source of help is even greater. The seller's banker will be less likely to use "puffery" to help the sale and will be interested in seeing a well-executed transaction.

The Computer

A recent source of help is computer-assisted analysis. Several software programs on the market can calculate ratios, construct comparative tables, and provide projections of sales, profit, and cash flow based on your plans.

The computer is most helpful in doing sensitivity analyses. These are the analyses that pose "what if" questions. The computer, and its software program, have the capability of calculating the total impact which would be caused by changes in the company (What if sales increase or decrease by 5 percent?). The calculations are done so quickly that you can probe nearly every variable of interest.

Three format worksheets are provided at the end of this chapter to help you capture data for your analyses:

Worksheet 12—"Income Statement Format"

Worksheet 13—"Balance Sheet Format"

Worksheet 14—"Source and Application of Funds Format"

At some point, you will decide you have enough knowledge to make your decision on whether to reject the candidate or proceed to make an offer. Before going on, it may be helpful to review all your work so far.

A Recap

Review

In Chapter 2, you took care of your benefits, selected your advisors, and did your preparation. Then, in Chapter 3, you took a personal inventory and established the criteria for your business. You made a tentative decision on what you can afford in Chapter 4, where you worked on how to value the business and how and where to get the money to buy it. In Chapter 5 you examined the alternative of starting a business. Armed with all this, you went and found the business in Chapter 6. In Chapter 7, you have done a great deal of analysis and, we will presume, you are ready to proceed to make an offer and negotiate the purchase.

Reconsider

Before you proceed, take the time to reconsider the whole idea of owning a business. Go back to Worksheet 1 and see whether your level of satisfaction will be significantly improved if you buy the business you are considering. Compare your life's situation under the two assumptions: You either own this business or you have a realistic job. Use a "plus and minus" list. If appropriate, involve your spouse.

Compare Income

Comparing the income from a job with the income from the business requires you to make some assumptions about the perquisites you will afford yourself. Any generous fringe benefits that might come from employment need to be carefully evaluated. Pension considerations may be important in your situation. Employment of family members and your personal tax situation will have an influence on this comparison.

Compare Wealth

Projecting your wealth may be difficult but it is important to do. The method to follow is to compare your total balance sheet under the same two assumptions of business ownership or employment. Prepare a personal balance sheet that reflects your present situation. Then prepare a balance sheet that projects your total assets and liabilities under the most probable assumptions about the performance of the business. Try to do the projection for 1 year and for 5 years. Repeat the projection of your balance sheet assuming that you have a job instead of the business.

Compare Satisfaction

You can only imagine some of the satisfactions and frustrations that will come from owning the business, so the comparison with employment, while necessary, is very subjective. Make your comparison by thinking through the things that affect satisfaction: family consideration, freedom, stress, risk, independence, working hours and conditions, intellectual stimulation, status and image, short- and long-term security, recognition, accomplishment, and the special element of obligation.

The obligations that come with business ownership might be viewed as the weight to be placed on the balance scale opposite the feelings of impotence that exist working for others. When working for others you are, de facto, subordinate. No matter how subtle or how abusive your treatment, you are subject to being told what to do and you are directly dependent on people you cannot avoid. When you own a business, you automatically incur obligations. The obligations are legal, financial, and in some cases, psychological. They exist 24 hours a day and are unavoidable—you can't just quit.

If you have alternatives other than owning a business or having a job, such as teaching, consulting, retirement, or government service, include these alternatives in this reconsideration.

Worksheet 11

A. Rating versus your business buying criteria (See Chapter 3 for review.) Use 1 to 10 scale; 10 is best.

Cash flow	_____	Growth potential	_____
Location	_____	Working conditions	_____
Liquidity	_____	Status and image	_____
People intensity	_____	Competition	_____
Overall desirability	_____	Content of the business	_____

Total _____ ÷ 10 = _____ Rating

B. Risk evaluation. (See Chapter 4 for review.) Use 1 to 6 scale; 6 is low risk.

Company history	_____	Special skills required	_____
The industry segment	_____	Special relationships required	_____
Location	_____	Labor situation	_____
Return *of* investment	_____	Management situation	_____
Return *on* investment	_____	Outside dependency	_____
Company reputation	_____	Products and services	_____
Competition	_____	Franchises/licenses required	_____
Technology	_____	Legal exposure	_____

Total _____ ÷ 16 = _____ Rating

Worksheet 12
Income Statement (P&L) Format
For the period _____ to _____

Sales $ _____
  Cost of sales $ _____
Gross profit $ _____

Expenses:
  Owner's salary $ _____
  Owner's benefits and taxes   _____
  Employee salaries (no. of people _____)   _____
  Employee benefits and taxes   _____
  Rent   _____
  Utilities   _____
  Travel and entertainment   _____
  Selling expenses   _____
  Depreciation   _____
  Insurance   _____
  Supplies   _____
  Interest   _____
  Automobile   _____
  Dues, licenses, subscriptions   _____
  Legal and accounting   _____
  Other _____   _____
  Other _____   _____
  Other _____   _____
Total expenses $ _____

Pre-tax profit $ _____

Worksheet 13
Balance Sheet Format

as of _____
Assets

Current assets:
  Cash $ _____
  Accounts receivable   _____
  Notes receivable   _____
  Inventory   _____
  Prepaid expenses   _____
  Other   _____
Total current assets $ _____

Fixed assets:
  Furniture, fixtures, machinery,
    and equipment $ _____
  Less: accumulated depreciation   _____ $ _____

  Land and buildings   _____
  Less: accumulated depreciation   _____ $ _____

Total fixed assets $ _____
Other assets _____   _____
Total assets $ _____

Liabilities and Owner's Equity

Current liabilities:
  Accounts payable $ _____
  Wages payable   _____
  Taxes payable   _____
  Interest payable   _____
  Notes/leases (current portion)   _____
  Services or products owed to customers   _____
  Other liabilities   _____
Total current liabilities $ _____

Long-term liabilities:
  Notes $ _____
  Mortgages   _____
  Other _____   _____
Total long-term liabilities $ _____

Owner's equity:
  Capital stock $ _____
  Retained earnings   _____

Total liabilities and owner's equity $ _____

Worksheet 14
Source and Application of Funds Format

Funds received from:

Profits	$ _____
Noncash expenses (i.e., depreciation)	_____
Increases in liabilities	_____
Decreases in assets (other than depreciation)	_____
Added equity	_____
Total funds received	$ _____

Funds applied to:

Losses	$ _____
Increases in assets	_____
Decreases in liabilities	_____
Payout of profit (dividends)	_____
Total funds applied	$ _____

8
Negotiating and Closing

The final sequence of events involves:

- Your offer, possibly followed by a series of counter offers
- An accepted offer, usually with some contingencies
- Your due diligence examination, and the satisfaction of the contingencies
- The drawing of the formal contract
- The closing

You will negotiate each of these steps, sometimes directly with the seller, sometimes through intermediaries. Worksheet 15 can help you stay organized. Appendix E contains a list of books on negotiating.

The Negotiations

Negotiating is the process whereby two parties who need or want something from each other reach a solution. The solution can be obtained through force, through compromise, through concessions, or some combination.

As an example, consider a buyer and seller who are far apart on the price of a business. If the seller has made a commitment to move out of the area in a short time and the buyer knows it, the buyer can exert economic force (take it or leave it). If the seller has no such pressure to leave, he or she might find a compromise with the buyer (split the difference). Or the buyer might agree to make a concession on the offered price if the seller will concede good terms of sale (this for that).

Effective negotiation has some natural enemies: fear, surprise, futility, and suspicion. The best defenses are facts, consistency, alternatives, and honesty. Being honest does not mean being naive or revealing how strongly you may want the business. It does mean you honestly want to buy the business, but you honestly can walk away. And, although there is no requirement for openness and candor, deception can be detrimental to negotiations. The discussion of negotiations which follows is based on 5 P's: perspective, preparation, posture, persuasion, and preservation.

Perspective

Perspective is needed to insure that the negotiations stay within the bounds of your personal values and your financial objectives. A key to gaining perspective is understanding that people act in their own perceived best interest. It doesn't matter that something may actually not be in a person's best interest; the important thing is it is perceived to be. A person's perception of reality is, after all, that person's reality.

A good way to maintain your perspective is to remain aware you do not have to buy this business. Now that you know how to find businesses, you can turn up other candidates. This doesn't mean you shouldn't be fully committed to working for the purchase of the right business. It does mean you should not pursue the business at any cost.

Your perspective should embrace the following facts about the business-buying negotiations:

- You don't have to buy the business.
- The seller may not have to sell to you.
- Negotiations will take longer than expected.
- There will be misunderstandings and things will go wrong.
- You may learn things during the negotiations that will change your position on some points.

Preparation

Preparation for negotiations involves learning as much as you can about the seller and the business. One fact has more impact on the negotiations than any other and cannot be emphasized enough—you must find out what the seller wants.

This is not as easy as it sounds. The seller may say one thing and mean another. The seller may not know. The seller may want things that appear irrational. You need to probe any answer you are given to learn the reasons the seller feels he or she wants something. You may uncover what the seller really wants. A typical example involves a seller who claims to want all-cash terms. If you probe for the reasons, you might hear "I want to retire and therefore I need all cash." The seller might be better off with a steady income from the higher price and extended interest-bearing terms you plan to offer.

Another common reason given is "I just want to walk away from the business with no worries; therefore I want all cash." Extending terms shouldn't have to mean any worries for the seller. You can provide excellent collateral. Perhaps the seller has worries about the business not being as sound as it's been represented.

The seller may want many things in some amount and some of these things may be contradictory:

- A high price
- All cash at closing
- Solid security
- Freedom from work
- Freedom from worry
- A reputation for getting a certain (high) price for the business
- Recognition
- A feeling of "winning"
- A stream of income or an annuity
- A quick deal
- A payment method to reward "potential"
- A continuing association
- Status
- A place to go and something to do
- Another business
- To get out from under this business
- Continued employment for friends or relatives
- Relief from debt
- Inclusion or exclusion of real estate

- To please a family member
- To buy or pay for something

The list is not complete but it illustrates how complex the issue can be.

The reason the seller's wants are so important to the negotiations is that they determine the structure the seller will find most acceptable. Knowing what the seller truly wants can permit you to develop creative alternatives. An example would be a seller who wants to retain ownership of the business real estate. The buyer wants the real estate and is prepared to pay full appraised value. By probing, the buyer finds out that the seller wants to keep the real estate to be able to have rental income. The buyer then develops the creative alternative of finding some other income-producing property for the seller to purchase. The seller gets the rental income and the buyer gets the business real estate.

Other preparation will have your advisors well informed and ready to support your efforts. Prepare alternative courses of action by presupposing what will happen. (If A happens, you will do one thing, but if B happens, you will do another.)

Posture

Posture has to do with your opening position, how the negotiations will be conducted (directly or through intermediaries), where any meetings will be held, and the tone and pace of the negotiations. A good clear posture helps to prevent surprises. Abrupt changes in the flow of negotiations can put the seller off balance, and, while that tactic may earn you some temporary advantage, it most often results in raising the seller's defenses against any future surprises.

Parties to negotiations sometimes adopt artificial postures to gain a negotiating advantage. Sellers may try to appear uninterested in selling or may give the impression several offers are pending. Buyers sometimes adopt a posture of offering an extremely low price and permit themselves to be brought up slowly as they gain other concessions. Other buyers offer a very high price which encourages the seller to make generous concessions and then reduce their offer as they find "problems."

Unless you are a very skilled negotiator or unless special circumstances exist, adopt a posture that is comfortable for you to maintain. To the extent you can, be cordial, polite, and businesslike. Be firm but patient. Be open for ideas and alert for opportunities to build toward a successful resolution. Recognize any "gamesmanship" for what it is and attempt to move the negotiations to a higher tone. Don't be rushed and don't be pressured.

The Offer

The centerpiece for the negotiations from this point on is the written offer. It should contain at least these elements:

- A description of what you are offering to purchase and the name(s) of the seller(s)
- The date of the offer and the date the offer expires
- The price
- The terms
- The interest rate, if any
- The repayment schedule, if any
- The amount of deposit, if any
- A date for closing
- The contingencies attached to your offer

Contingencies. There are two kinds of contingencies. One kind makes the offer subject to the occurrence of some activities. The offer may be contingent on an examination of the books and records or the assignment of the lease. The second kind of contingency makes the offer subject to the existence of certain conditions. For example, the offer may be contingent upon the level of inventory or the value of certain assets.

Contingencies are put into an offer to break a typical log jam in negotiations. On one hand, the buyer can't make an intelligent offer without facts about the business. On the other, the seller doesn't want to open up the confidential details about the business to someone who may not buy it. The solution has become the contingent offer. The seller provides information to the buyer but does not allow the buyer to review the books, talk to employees, or the like. The seller provides enough information to enable the buyer to make a decision and develop an offer.

The buyer submits an offer based on the information provided by the seller but reserves the right to withdraw the offer, cancel any agreements, and have the deposit returned if, upon examination by the buyer, the information is not correct or certain conditions are not met. This examination is called due diligence.

The wording of the contingent conditions is very important. Buyers would like to have the contingencies as broad as possible so that any decision to buy or not buy is within their control. An example of a broad contingency is "all financial data is subject to examination and approval by the buyer's accountant." The practical impact of this statement is to give the buyer complete access to the financial records with no obligation to complete the deal. The accountant just has to "disapprove" the financial data.

Sellers want the contingencies very narrow so that they are clearly identifiable and easy to meet. A narrow contingency would be "this offer is subject only to the buyer's verification that sales, costs, and expenses were as shown on the financial statements given to the buyer."

Your contingencies should cover anything critical to your decision. Verification of financial data is almost always needed. If certain employees or customers are essential, your contingencies can include satisfactory agreements with them. The same applies to contracts with key suppliers or the franchisor, if there is one.

The most common contingency involves the future rent or purchase of the business location. If your decision to buy the business is based on your assuming the present lease or renegotiating other arrangements, you should establish such a contingency in your offer (see Figure 8.1). If you are going to borrow money to buy the business, you might want to make your offer subject to your ability to obtain financing.

Word your contingencies so that you have the right to withdraw your offer but not the obligation to withdraw. Your contingencies may not be met, but you still may want to go forward. The offer, with all its terms and contingencies, is both critical and complex enough to warrant review by your advisors.

Persuasion

Persuasion is convincing another to accept or do something. But if, as we've said, people only do things they perceive to be in their own best interest, you need to show how what you want is in the seller's best interest.

Just as you have the obligation to find out what the seller wants, the seller has an obligation to learn what you want. If the seller hasn't been alert enough to ask you, you have to tell him or her. An opening negotiating dialogue between you and the seller can be a factual review of your offer and the reasons for it. Get the seller to invest time in understanding your offer. It's a way to get the seller participating in a solution.

Learn from Rejection.   Be ready to have almost any opening offer rejected and learn all you can from the experience. Get the reasons for it. Determine the key points in the seller's arguments. Keep asking "why" so that you can understand what is behind the objections. Do not argue

If you are entering into a real estate lease, take the time to understand this important transaction. Above all, if you are planning to take over the seller's lease, review it personally with your attorney early in the negotiations. There are several reasons for reviewing the lease in detail as soon as possible:

- Sellers don't always remember the terms and conditions or the revisions to them.
- The seller may have changed the use of the premises or the hours of operation to something not allowed. The landlord may not be aware of it.
- The lease, its assignability, or its renewability may be legally flawed.
- While the lease may appear assignable, it is still usually subject to the landlord's approval. While the lease may say that the landlord may "not unreasonably withhold approval," landlords sometimes try to extract higher rent by threatening to withhold or delay approval.
- The terms of responsibility for taxes, maintenance, and insurance need to be understood. The difference between a rate quoted "gross" (the three items are included) or quoted "triple net" (the three items are paid additionally by the tenant) can be significant.
- Whether you are entering into a new lease or assuming an existing one, do not be intimidated by the rigid boilerplate language in a standardized lease form. You should negotiate for the best terms and conditions you can obtain.
- Lease negotiations involve attorneys and take time to complete.

The lease you are able to negotiate may make the difference between a viable business transaction and one you should avoid.

Figure 8.1. Negotiating the lease.

your position yet. Just present your offer and make sure it is understood. Then wring every bit of intelligence you can from the rejection. At some point, ask for a counteroffer. Once you have a counteroffer, you can develop more specific negotiating tactics.

Use Concessions. Assess where you are far apart and where you are near agreement. Develop a list of things you can give (concessions) and a list of concessions the seller could give. Think of as many alternatives as possible to give the seller what he or she wants. Think of alternatives for the seller to give you what you want. Restructure a new offer which reflects the sum of your understanding. This time, you do argue your points.

Price—The Common Stumbling Block. Because price is the most common area of difference, we will use it as our example. The seller may view the price of the business as a reflection of his or her worth. It's common for owners to think of their businesses as extensions of themselves. They will say "all those years of hard work should be worth at least this much." You may have to point out that all those years of hard work provided a fine living, a nice home, and so on. The selling price of the business is only the residual value of the seller's work.

Sellers sometime base their price on cash taken from the business but never shown on the books. (An admission of tax evasion is not a particularly good testimonial to the seller's honesty.) Whether the cash ever really existed or not, don't accept any pricing logic that cannot be proven.

If the seller does have a genuine logic for the price, find out what it is. Understand it and let the seller know you understand it. Then you can ask for understanding of your pricing logic. If you based your price primarily on the value of the assets, ask for the seller's help to know why it should be otherwise. If you used a capitalization rate on the cash flow as your pricing method, explain your method to the seller and ask to know how you can be more correct.

You may want to compare the seller's price to the cost of duplicating the business. Review with the seller what the cost would be to start a similar business. Let the seller find any flaws in your logic. You might say "help me understand why your price is correct when it would cost so much less to start a similar business".

Keep Your Argument Centered.   Your persuasion should always return to the central proposition that your offer is in the seller's best interest. Here is a simple technique: point out that you want to pay a fair price and one which will allow you to afford to buy the business. Your objective is to buy the business and a fair, affordable price is in the seller's best interest because it facilitates the sale.

Be Ready for the Worst.   Unfortunately, negotiations don't always flow along as logically as our example. Outbursts of temper, seller regret, ego needs, ill-conceived positions, and almost any other vagary of human nature can turn the negotiations into an emotionally charged circus. A competent intermediary can buffer these frictions and defuse problems before they get out of hand. Your strategy when confronted with an emotional situation should be to acknowledge the other person's strong feelings and begin at once to focus away from personalities and motives and toward a range of solutions.

No detailed script can be written to cover all the variations you will encounter. Use your list of concessions from both sides to persuade the seller to move toward agreement. Use your advisors as sounding boards and sources of creative strategies and tactics.

Preservation

Preservation of your negotiations involves building upon agreements and narrowing areas of disagreement. It involves keeping the negotiations progressing through the stresses and strains that are bound to occur. It means preventing every difference from threatening the whole negotiation and causing it to fall apart.

Poor negotiators and those who rely on power techniques often refer to a particular issue as a "deal breaker." What they mean is that the issue is important. Their overly dramatic reference is intended to put pressure on the other party. The result all too often is to put the negotiations generally on thin ice where any issue can become a deal breaker and no foundation for progress can be built. There may be a time for the dramatic, but negotiations which progress on solid gains stand a much better chance of success. There are several books listed in Appendix E which can give you a thorough grounding in negotiation.

The Closing

When negotiations are successful and an agreement is reached, a process for closing the transaction is set up. A formal contract containing all the facts of the agreement needs to be drawn. The seller's attorney usually prepares the first version for review by the buyer and his or her attorney. If you have not yet done your due diligence examination, now is the time.

Due Diligence

The term "due diligence" properly infers an obligation on your part to satisfy yourself regarding the facts of the business. The seller allows you to examine records, books, facilities, contracts, and, if your offer contains such contingencies, to talk with employees, customers, suppliers, and others. Your objective is to determine if the information you relied upon to decide to buy the business is correct. If your offer was well written, it provides you with a way to cancel your agreement if certain information is not proven to be true. Use your advisors and the analytical techniques provided earlier. Your due diligence may result in the withdrawal or revision of your offer if the facts prove to be different from what you were given.

Once your contingencies are satisfied and the contract is in its final form, you can close. The closing is the formal transfer of the business or its assets to you. Unlike a real estate closing, in which the routines are well known and commonly, if not always smoothly, executed, business closings are seldom routine. Each business and the terms of its sale are unique. Even your advisors may not be thoroughly familiar with the intricacies of a business sale.

The best way to insure a smooth closing is to set up a checklist. Things may still go wrong, but you will have a blueprint to follow. Where it is appropriate, each item on the checklist should be assigned to someone. More than one closing has been put off because no one got a copy of the lease.

The Checklist

The agreement you reached with the seller spelled out the key points of the arrangement. As the formal contracts get hammered out, more and more details get covered. Some of the items in the checklist in Figure 8.2 may be included in the contract; others are just reminders of things that need to be done.

The Twilight Time.   An important item on the checklist covers what will happen during the time between contract signing and the closing. The time between the two events can be weeks or months. You might be waiting for your financing or the seller may be waiting for an up-to-date appraisal. Whatever the reason, provisions have to be made for how the business is to be conducted during that time. Typically, the seller agrees to operate the business in its customary way. You may want to spell out specific dos and don'ts, especially as they relate to *prices*—a big discount price sale can bring in quick money, deplete inventory, and load up customers; *purchasing*—failing to buy needed goods and supplies can conserve the seller's cash but leave you in a bad opening position; and *people*—hiring and firing at this stage can create real problems for you as you learn the new business.

Asset Sale versus Stock Sale.   Another important item on the checklist is to decide on the method of sale. In most cases, the sale method will be a sale of assets. The assets are identified and title is passed, usually with some warranties such as the collectability of the accounts receivable and the quality of the inventory. If liabilities are to be assumed, they are carefully defined.

- Conduct of the business until closing
- The time and place of closing
- A list of everyone who needs to attend
- A list of all the documents required
- A breakdown of the funds to be disbursed
- Absolute assurance that the funds are available in the amount and form specified
- Your new corporate tax and employer identification numbers
- Provision for any licenses to be obtained or transferred
- Pro-rationing calculations for taxes, wages, utility bills, etc.
- Adjustments for any deposits the seller may have with the landlord, suppliers, or utilities
- Transfer of banking arrangements
- Transfer of keys and alarm codes
- Transfer of any computer codes
- The real estate lease or purchase agreement
- Customer lists
- Transfer of utilities, particularly the telephone number
- Any separate contracts establishing seller's obligations to consult or to not compete
- Allocation of the selling price to assets, consulting, noncompete agreement, and goodwill
- Provision for broker's fees
- Clearance of outstanding liens or encumbrances
- Compliance with bulk sales laws to notify suppliers
- Assumption or discharge of any other leases or mortgages
- Definition of the warranties and guarantees the seller will provide
- Provision for security by the buyer
- Definition of the seller's obligations to help in the transition of the business and training of the buyer
- Adjustments for actual inventory and receivables value at closing
- Adjustments in the event that accounts receivable are not collected
- Disposition of any outstanding claims or litigation against or by the seller
- Provision for continuity of insurance or bonding

Figure 8.2. The closing checklist.

The alternative method is a stock sale, in which the buyer purchases the shares of stock of a business. Under some conditions, there are advantages to a stock sale. If the company has tax losses to carry forward, a favorable lease, or other important contracts or if the assets of the business are encumbered, a stock sale may be the method to use. The big risk with purchasing the stock of a corporation is that you are also purchasing all liabilities, both known *and unknown.* A lawsuit over some past activity by the company could prove to be a most unwelcome and expensive surprise. If the advantages are worth using the stock sale method, you can attempt to get the seller to indemnify you for any claims that may be made. The importance of these actions and the changing legal and tax environment make having competent advice essential throughout this phase.

Allocating the Selling Price.   The price you are paying for the business can be allocated among different items of value. For example, a portion of the price may be allocated to the purchase of the assets. Another portion may be paid out under a consulting agreement with the seller. Yet another portion of the price may be paid as consideration for the seller's agreement not to compete with you for some period of time in your market.

Tax considerations influence these allocations. Under the old tax laws the seller wanted the whole selling price allocated to the purchase of the assets. This meant that the entire premium over the value of the assets would be taxed to the seller as capital gains at a much lower rate than ordinary income at that time.

The buyer wanted as small a premium as possible over the value of the assets because that amount would be considered "good will" and could not be depreciated for tax purposes. The buyer would ask the seller to accept some portion of the purchase price as payment for a covenant not to compete and some portion as a consulting fee. These payments are considered expenses by the buyer and ordinary income for the seller. The new owner would be able to fully deduct these payments as expenses, but the seller would have to pay the (then) higher ordinary income tax rates.

While the new tax laws effectively erase the difference in tax rates, there are still reasons, primarily to do with goodwill, for you and your advisors to carefully allocate the purchase price.

Manage Your Closing.   The purpose of the checklist is to insure that, after all your hard work to find and buy the business, some glitch doesn't develop. A tantrum at the closing table over some mistake or omission is the last thing you want now. Unfortunately, it happens all too often as people underestimate the complexity of the transaction. Your management of the closing can be your first management task as a business owner.

Worksheet 15
Negotiation Data Sheet

Telephone

A. People	Name/Address	Business	Home
Seller			
Seller's attorney			
Seller's accountant			
Your attorney			
Your accountant			
Broker			
Other			
Other			
Other			

B. What the seller wants most

1. _____ 2. _____ 3. _____

C. Opening positions

Item	Seller	Buyer
Price		
Cash down payment		
Terms:		
Years		
Interest rate		
Other		
Other		

D. Possible Concessions

Seller could concede:	Buyer could concede:
1. _____	1. _____
2. _____	2. _____
3. _____	3. _____
4. _____	4. _____
5. _____	5. _____

9

When the Business Is a Franchise

Whether you are buying an existing franchised location from a franchisee or a new location from the franchisor, there are some special procedures to follow.

What Is a Franchise?

A franchise is a license. In most cases, it is a license to use a franchisor's name and to offer its products or services for sale in exchange for certain fees. The terms of the license are spelled out in a franchise agreement.

The Franchise Agreement

This agreement will cover in detail the obligations that you and the franchisor have to each other. It will include such things as:

- *The price of the franchise, the terms of any financing, and the ongoing royalty schedule.*
- *A list of exactly what you are getting for your money.* In addition to the right to use the franchisor's name and to sell the products or services, you may be getting training, certain equipment, a starting inventory, special promotions, or a number of other things.
- *The procedures you must follow in operating the franchise.* Some franchises have very detailed manuals that cover all aspects of oper-

139

ations, from what color uniforms are required to how to clean the floors. Some franchises permit a degree of flexibility; others require strict adherence to procedures. All require some form of reporting and controls.

- *The duration of the agreement and the procedures governing sale, renewal, and transfer.* Also covered are the conditions under which either side may cancel the agreement.

- *A definition of the territory.* Your territory may be narrow or broad, exclusive or unprotected, or some combination which might even change over time.

- *A definition of the responsibilities for operations.* The agreement covers the responsibility for pricing, purchasing, advertising, paying invoices, hiring, training, insurance coverage, maintenance, security, and similar items. Some franchisors require the franchisee to personally operate their franchise. If the franchisor provides consulting or trouble-shooting support, it should be covered in the agreement.

- *The plan for the facility.* Some franchisors provide the complete facility, others give detailed specifications, and others offer little or no guidance. Some franchisors own the facility and lease it to the franchisee. In other cases, the facility is rented from a landlord—sometimes from the franchisee.

The franchise agreement is an imposing document which your attorney should review for you.

The Pluses of a Franchise

The most obvious benefit provided by a franchise is an established, tested product or service. Equally important can be the methods and systems which have been refined to a smooth set of procedures and which have been proven successful. You are able to benefit from the franchisor's learning curve.

The strong franchisor is almost certainly able to secure a better location than an individual. The franchisor has more technical expertise in site selection and has more financial clout to negotiate and sign up good locations.

If the franchisor is a heavy advertiser and promoter, the recognition factor can be a big plus for the franchisee. The economy of scale available to the franchisor can permit advertising on television and other media that is too expensive for the independent operator. Economies of scale may extend to purchasing of materials and supplies, giving you lower prices than you could obtain on your own.

Training, consulting, and any other help the franchisor provides can be very meaningful. The independent operator has limited and often expensive resources for help. If you came from a large organization, you may appreciate the availability of the franchisor's field staff.

If you are buying a franchise direct from the franchisor, not a resale, you will have no complicated analyses of past operations to conduct. You will, in effect, have a clean slate.

The Minuses of a Franchise

The restrictions and controls imposed by the franchisor are the greatest drawbacks to a franchised business. The ongoing royalties can seem onerous, particularly if franchisor support is weak. The ownership of the franchise license is not permanent. This could pose a serious problem later on. The franchisor's management and financial strength may become weak or may fail. You could be adversely affected by events outside your control. You may be prohibited from expanding or relocating your business because of the franchisor's licensing of others. If the franchisor requires you to purchase its products and supplies and does not permit you to buy on the open market, you may pay uncompetitive prices.

If the Franchise Is a Resale

Buying a franchise resale is like buying any other business, but it requires some additional steps. You will need to get the approval of the franchisor. In most cases, you will be asked to submit a financial statement and your plan for the business. Provision will have to be made for your training. You will have to familiarize yourself with and accept all the terms and conditions of the franchise agreement and the requirements which it places on your operating procedures. You may have to be interviewed as a part of the franchisor's acceptance procedure.

While these may seem to be added burdens, there is one step which is only possible when buying a franchise: You have the ability to talk to the owners of similar businesses. Talking with other franchisees can give you information and insights unavailable to you with other businesses. You can get the first-hand experiences of people who own, manage, and work a business very similar to the one you are considering.

The balance of your investigation, analysis, negotiations, and closing will be very similar to those outlined in the preceding chapter.

If the Franchise Is a New Location

There are several major differences between buying an ongoing business and a new franchise location. We will use the outline of this book to examine some of these differences.

Deciding What You Want

In deciding what you want (Chapter 3), there are some new choices to make if you are considering franchises. We mentioned existing versus new franchises, but within the new franchises you may find choices. If you are considering a fast food business, there are franchises featuring pizza, hamburger, and all kinds of sandwiches. Even if you have narrowed your choice, say to quick printing, there are several franchises from which to choose.

Determining What You Can Afford

Determining what you can afford (Chapter 4) requires a new approach because you do not have historical financial data to analyze and you don't have to go through the complications of pricing the business. The complication you do face is the requirement to deal with projections of future financial performance. No reputable franchisor will guarantee what your results will be. You will be forced to make judgments and take risks on your own evaluation of the franchise and the location.

Of course, you do have a unique source of help which was mentioned earlier—the owners of other franchise locations. You can ask the other owners how close to projection they came. You can learn about the problems and any surprises these owners encountered.

You can also ask about any flexibility the franchisor might have with regard to price and terms.

Finding the Business

Finding the business (Chapter 6) is actually a little easier with a franchise. If you know which one you want, you can contact that franchise directly.

If you don't know, you have all the sources presented in Chapter 6 plus some new ones:

Franchise Opportunities Handbook, Superintendent of Documents, U.S. Government Printing Office, Washington, DC 20402

Membership Directory (and other publications), International Franchise Association, Suite 1005, 1025 Connecticut Ave., NW, Washington, DC 20036

Directory of Franchising Organizations, Pilot Books, 347 Fifth Avenue, New York, NY 10016

Analyzing the Business

Analyzing the business (Chapter 7) is the step that will be the most different when the business is a franchise. The whole process of learning about the seller and finding out what he or she wants is not relevant to a franchise.

The Disclosure Document. Franchisors are required to publish a disclosure document that will give you more information than you can ever hope to get from a business owner. It covers:

- The description of the franchise
- The franchisor's ownership and financial condition
- Background data on key people
- The price, royalties, territory, and other terms of the franchise license (including any financing which may be available)
- The operational duties of the franchisee
- Any other obligations of the franchisor, such as training, advertising, and promotion
- The procedures for sale, repurchase, default, termination, renewal, and transfer of the franchise.
- The procedure to establish the physical location
- Any litigation in which the franchisor is or has been involved
- Any restrictions on purchases or sales by the franchisee
- Information about past, present, and projected franchisee locations including, where appropriate, the names of the franchisees.

Other Franchisees. It is this last item that can help you locate other franchisees. You can get valuable insights into the franchisor's behavior and performance by talking with people who have had first-hand experience. You can find out if promises were kept and how the quality of the goods, services, training, and other support compared to what was expected.

If you can locate the former owners of failed locations, you may be able to get some very useful, although possibly tainted, insights into the downside risks of the franchise.

The Franchisor.   Of course, the franchisor itself is the prime source of information. You may be subjected to a high-pressure sales approach or you may have to initiate the contact, but either way, there is plenty of information available.

The franchisor will want information about you, too. References, a summary of your experience, and your financial statement are a minimum. You may also be asked to prepare a business plan to demonstrate your ability to manage the franchise.

Judgment Required.   Your real job in buying a franchise is to exercise good judgment on all the information you will have.

- Is the franchise a good value? What are you getting that you couldn't provide for yourself or obtain by buying a nonfranchise for the same price?

- Is the franchisor reputable and financially stable? Are the people competent and trustworthy?

- Do you have confidence that the financial projections you have developed are realistic and achievable? The key element in the projections is the market potential.

- Does this franchise satisfy the basic criteria and does it meet the risk preferences you established in Chapter 3?

Franchising is a dynamic field. More and more kinds of businesses are available as franchises. No search for your business should be considered complete unless you have investigated the franchise opportunities.

Epilogue
The First Month
of Ownership

Your objective in the early days of your ownership is to take control of your new business. Immerse yourself and learn.

Make Changes Slowly

Because you can't know all the critical interdependencies in the business yet, be careful about making sweeping or dramatic changes. If you were to change the name of the business, you might lose old customers. You might change some supplier only to find that supplier's brother is (or was) your biggest customer. If the business is on a fairly even keel, take things slowly.

Put Out Fires. Of course, if you are faced with serious problems, you must take some action. If the crisis involves relationships with other people such as customers, employees, creditors and so on, a new owner can often buy time by listening to the issue, acknowledging the concern, and demonstrating a sincere intent to resolve the problem. Most reasonable people will give a new owner time to learn the facts and come back with a proposed solution.

No matter what the crisis, you can usually find some help. Everyone around you has a stake in your success, including the former owner. The former owner may have a special interest in your success if you owe him or her money. There may be the case when you have to decide alone, but that's why you wanted your own business.

Learn the Routines and the Culture. Every business has its own flow and rhythms. Even if you think you want to change it, learn the culture you bought. The small secrets contained in everyday actions may be the keys to success or the barriers to progress.

Focus on People

Your first days should be full of people contact. No matter how trite it sounds, people are what business is mostly about. Human skills, needs, and resources form the basis for production of any kind. In all your people contact, be searching for their views on the key opportunities and threats to your business.

Employees.   Get to know your people. Learn their skills and knowledge. Determine if they are satisfied or not and why. Set up a communications pattern that you can sustain. Harm can be done if you start a program of heavy communication and then withdraw. As important as it is to listen to your people, it's also important for you to talk to them. They will want to get to know you. You are an important person in their lives and what you plan to do affects them very much. To the extent you can, offer reassurance that nothing harmful to them is imminent.

Customers.   How successful you are at communicating with customers may very well determine how successful your business will be. Because you now control what your company does, you have the power to satisfy your customers. Listening to their needs and comments is a top-priority activity. Find a way to build an ongoing dialogue.

Suppliers.   New owners sometimes overlook these important people. To one extent or another, you do rely on them. Their success already depends on your success, so look for ways to make them part of your business team.

Bankers, Lenders, and Investors.   A big fear many new business owners have is that their banker or investor will try to interfere with the business. To try to prevent this intrusion, new owners sometimes do the worst thing possible—they try to keep these people out of the business and in the dark. The best course of action is to find out what your lenders and investors expect from you and try to give it to them. If they know you are performing, they will usually stay out of your way. If you do get into trouble, they will want to help.

Advisors.   You will need to develop your working relationships with your advisors. Your accountant is a very key person. You may also find you need some specialized advice from consultants or others. Seminars and books are available on topics ranging from personnel hiring and training to advertising to negotiating with vendors. Be prepared to learn that, no matter what kind of advice you need, the chances are that someone is out there to sell it to you.

Set Simple Controls

At the early stages of your ownership you need to decide which few critical factors could cause major damage or possible failure for your business. Once you identify them, you can establish controls. Controls may be needed on cash, quality, expenses, purchasing, or some area of employee performance, for example. In the beginning, pick only the most important factors and try to keep the controls easy to administer.

Learn How to Measure Results

You may be surprised at how results are really measured in smaller companies. While financial results are the final measure, they are incomplete and the reports are available only long after they can do much good. The true indicators of results may be the number of phone calls per day or the labor hours per unit or the number of days backlog in the order book. Every business has measures of productivity that will predict results. Find out what they are in your new business and begin tracking your progress.

Define Key Opportunities and Threats

Whether or not you actively develop a formal business plan will depend on your philosophy about planning and the requirements of your lenders and investors. Regardless of what you think of business plans, you should at least define the key opportunities and threats your business faces. You were urged to review this subject in your discussions with employees, customers, and others. If your business is part of an association, get its views. Ask for ideas from your Chamber of Commerce and neighboring businesses.

Conclusion

You are about to take the steps which will lead to owning your own business, with all the rewards and responsibilities which go with it. You will be the one who will have to bring everything together. You will have to find, analyze, negotiate, finance, and buy the business. By that time, you will learn the lesson which all new business owners learn—nothing happens unless you make it happen.

Standard Industrial Classification Codes

Number of Business Establishments by State

Code state	Post office abbreviation	Number of business establishments
01 Alabama	AL	69,099
03 Alaska	AK	15,629
05 Arizona	AZ	85,650
07 Arkansas	AR	53,623
09 California	CA	630,591
11 Colorado	CO	88,884
13 Connecticut	CT	83,438
15 Delaware	DE	13,191
16 District of Columbia	DC	19,968
17 Florida	FL	271,985
19 Georgia	GA	125,346
21 Hawaii	HI	23,366
23 Idaho	ID	25,368
25 Illinois	IL	277,375
27 Indiana	IN	111,822
29 Iowa	IA	74,224
31 Kansas	KS	71,921
33 Kentucky	KY	77,999
35 Louisiana	LA	94,903
37 Maine	ME	26,843
39 Maryland	MD	90,136
41 Massachusetts	MA	137,743
43 Michigan	MI	195,941
45 Minnesota	MN	113,931
47 Mississippi	MS	47,115

(Continued)

Code state	Post office abbreviation	Number of business establishments
49 Missouri	MO	123,328
51 Montana	MT	27,945
53 Nebraska	NE	48,043
55 Nevada	NV	22,136
57 New Hampshire	NH	24,682
59 New Jersey	NJ	183,833
61 New Mexico	NM	30,799
63 New York	NY	432,524
65 North Carolina	NC	117,125
67 North Dakota	ND	19,210
69 Ohio	OH	229,601
71 Oklahoma	OK	85,386
73 Oregon	OR	73,235
75 Pennsylvania	PA	260,323
77 Rhode Island	RI	23,537
79 South Carolina	SC	58,574
81 South Dakota	SD	20,463
83 Tennessee	TN	90,840
85 Texas	TX	392,012
87 Utah	UT	36,442
89 Vermont	VT	13,990
91 Virginia	VA	105,308
93 Washington	WA	112,489
95 West Virginia	WV	31,876
97 Wisconsin	WI	114,771
99 Wyoming	WY	15,634

Standard Industrial Classification (SIC)

The Standard Industrial Classification, commonly referred to as the SIC code, was developed by the U.S. Government in conjunction with U.S. business. It divides virtually all economic activity into ten major divisions:

Agriculture, Forestry, and Fishing	01–09
Mining	10–14
Construction	15–17
Manufacturing	20–39
Transportation, Communication and Public Utilities	40–49
Wholesale Trade	50–51
Retail Trade	52–59
Finance, Insurance, & Real Estate Services	60–67

| Business Services | 70–89 |
| Health/Social Services, and Public Administration | 91–97 |

The SIC categorizes businesses into one of these ten division and assigns it a third and fourth digit for further identification. The identification can be very narrow and specific.

20	Manufacturing—Food
202	Manufacturing—Dairy products
2024	Manufacturing—Ice cream and frozen deserts

As a business seeker, the SIC system can show you:

1. How many companies there are in any given category.
2. Where they are.
3. How large they are in terms of employment and sales.

Standard Industrial Classification (SIC) Listing

Numerical Order

Note: The following list of business establishments by category includes both the primary and secondary SIC's for all lines of business:

SIC DESCRIPTION	NO. OF ESTAB.
AGRICULTURE, FORESTRY & FISHING	201,534
01 Agricultural Production—Crops	86,436
0111 Wheat	7,506
0112 Rice	1,687
0115 Corn	7,556
0116 Soybeans	6,560
0119 Cash Grains, nec	6,984
0131 Cotton	3,450
0132 Tobacco	730
0133 Sugar Crops	712
0134 Potatoes, Irish	1,329
0139 Field Crops Except Cash Grains, nec	3,359
0161 Vegetables & Melons	4,437
0171 Berry Crops	889
0172 Grapes	1,407
0173 Tree Nuts	876
0174 Citrus Fruits	1,570

SIC DESCRIPTION	NO. OF ESTAB.
0175 Deciduous Tree Fruits	3,268
0179 Fruits & Tree Nuts, nec	513
0181 Nursery Products, Ornamental	12,386
0182 Food Crops Grown Undercover	1,040
0189 Horticulture Specialties, nec	205
0191 Farm Crops, General	19,972
02 Agricultural Production—Livestock	43,897
0211 Beef Cattle Feedlots	3,040
0212 Beef Cattle Except Feedlots	16,053
0213 Hogs	4,376
0214 Sheep & Goats	683
0219 General Livestock	687
0241 Dairy Farms	8,013
0251 Fowls, Broilers & Fryers	807
0252 Chicken Eggs	1,528
0253 Turkeys & Turkey Eggs	527
0254 Poultry Hatcheries	783
0259 Poultry & Eggs, nec	205
0271 Fur-bearing Animals & Rabbits	481
0272 Horses & Other Equine	2,021
0279 Animal Specialties, nec	2,616
0291 Farms, Primarily Livestock	2,077
07 Agricultural Services	66,794
0711 Soil Preparation Services	1,450
0721 Crop Planting & Protection	3,781
0722 Crop Harvesting	2,006
0723 Crop Preparation Services for Market	3,911
0724 Cotton Ginning	1,831
0729 Crop Services, General	375
0741 Veterinarian Services, Farm Stock	2,086
0742 Veterinarian Services, Specialties	9,735
0751 Livestock Services	2,302
0752 Animal Specialty Services	5,283
0761 Farm Labor Contractor	343
0762 Farm Management Services	841
0781 Landscape Counseling	11,706
0782 Lawn & Garden Services	16,744
0783 Shrub & Tree Services	4,400
08 Forestry	2,102
0811 Timber Tracts	1,026
0821 Forest Nurseries & Tree Seed	168
0843 Extraction Pine Gum	8
0849 Forest Products, Gathering of, nec	51
0851 Forestry Services	849
09 Fishing, Hunting & Trapping	2,305
0912 Finfish	849
0913 Shellfish	1,010
0919 Marine Products, Misc.	28
0921 Fish Hatcheries & Preserves	283
0971 Hunting & Trapping Game Propagation	135
MINING	56,028
10 Metal Mining	2,521

SIC DESCRIPTION	NO. OF ESTAB.
1011 Iron Ores	130
1021 Copper Ores	136
1031 Lead, Zinc Ores	118
1041 Gold Ores	702
1044 Silver Ores	443
1051 Bauxite, Aluminum Ores	30
1061 Ferroalloy Ores	84
1081 Metal Mining Services	531
1092 Mercury Ores	7
1094 Uranium-Radium Ores	238
1099 Metal Ores, nec	102
11 Anthracite Mining	291
1111 Anthracite	247
1112 Anthracite Mining Services	44
12 Bituminous Coal & Lignite Mining	4,966
1211 Bituminous Coal & Lignite	4,218
1213 Bituminous, Lignite, Mining Services	748
13 Oil & Gas Extraction	42,205
1311 Crude Oil & Natural Gas	17,667
1321 Natural Gas Liquids	217
1381 Drilling Oil & Gas Wells	6,503
1382 Oil, Gas Exploration Services	5,372
1389 Oil, Gas Field Services, nec	12,446
14 Nonmetallic Minerals, Except Fuels	6,045
1411 Dimension Stone	282
1422 Limestone, Crushed & Broken	1,190
1423 Granite, Crushed & Broken	95
1429 Stone, Crushed & Broken, nec	342
1442 Construction Sand & Gravel	2,601
1446 Industrial Sand	168
1452 Bentonite	47
1453 Fire Clay	37
1454 Fuller's Earth	11
1455 Kaolin, Ball Clay	57
1459 Clay & Related Minerals, nec	112
1472 Barite	47
1473 Fluorspar	19
1474 Potash, Soda & Borate Minerals	46
1475 Phosphate Rock	49
1476 Rock Salt	28
1477 Sulfur	21
1479 Chemical and Fertilizer Mining, nec	36
1481 Nonmetallic Minerals (Except Fuels) Services	237
1492 Gypsum	46
1496 Talc, Soapstone and Pyrophyllite	27
1499 Nonmetallic Minerals, nec	547
CONSTRUCTION	836,960
15 General Building Contractors	341,407
1521 Single Family Housing Construction	185,303
1522 Residential Construction	25,518
1531 Operative Builders	36,360
1541 Industrial Buildings & Warehouses	22,320

SIC DESCRIPTION	NO. OF ESTAB.
1542 Nonresidential Construction	71,906
16 Heavy Construction Contractors	50,385
1611 Highway & Street Construction	18,848
1622 Bridge, Tunnel & Elevated Highway	2,582
1623 Water Sewer & Utility	14,517
1629 Heavy Construction, nec	14,438
17 Special Trade Contractors	445,168
1711 Plumbing, Heating (Except Electrical) & Air Conditioning	103,616
1721 Painting, Paper Hanging & Decorations	31,614
1731 Electrical Work	72,797
1741 Masonry, Other Stonework	17,478
1742 Plastering, Drywall, Insulation	21,420
1743 Terrazzo, Tile, Marble & Mosaic Work	6,299
1751 Carpentering	20,031
1752 Floor Laying, Floor Work, nec	15,299
1761 Roofing, Sheet Metal Work	33,176
1771 Concrete Work	18,680
1781 Water Well Drilling	5,863
1791 Structural Steel Erection	5,423
1793 Glass, Glazing Work	7,778
1794 Excavating & Foundation Work	36,451
1795 Wrecking, Demolition Work	2,197
1796 Installation, Building Equipment, nec	3,342
1799 Special Trade Contractors, nec	43,704
MANUFACTURING	592,994
20 Food & Kindred Products	32,718
2011 Meat Packing Plants	2,863
2013 Sausages & Other Prepared Meat	1,871
2016 Poultry Dressing Plant	374
2017 Poultry & Egg Processing	276
2021 Butter	211
2022 Cheese, Natural & Processed	901
2023 Milk, Condensed & Evaporated	317
2024 Ice Cream & Frozen Dessert	991
2026 Milk, Fluid	1,040
2032 Canned Specialties	371
2033 Canned Fruits, Vegetables & Related Products	1,200
2034 Dried & Dehydrated Fruits, Vegetables & Related	288
2035 Pickled Fruits & Vegetables, Sauces & Salad Dressings	774
2037 Frozen Fruits & Vegetables	404
2038 Frozen Specialties	622
2041 Flour & Grain Mill Products	599
2043 Cereal Preparations	111
2044 Rice Milling	90
2045 Flour, Blended & Prepared	227
2046 Wet Corn Milling	127
2047 Pet Food, Dog, Cat & Other	415
2048 Prepared Feeds, nec	2,451
2051 Bread, Cake & Related Products	2,958
2052 Cookies & Crackers	653
2061 Sugar, Raw Cane	78
2062 Sugar Refining, Cane	55

SIC DESCRIPTION	NO. OF ESTAB.
2063 Sugar, Beet	61
2065 Confectionery Products	1,521
2066 Chocolate & Cocoa Products	224
2067 Chewing Gum	30
2074 Cottonseed Oil Mills	101
2075 Soybean Oil Mills	151
2076 Vegetable Oil Mills	76
2077 Animal & Marine Fats & Oils	369
2079 Lard & Cooking Oils, nec	201
2082 Malt Liquors	143
2083 Malt	50
2084 Wine, Brandy & Brandy Spirits	830
2085 Distilled & Blended Liquor Except Brandy	180
2086 Soft Drinks, Bottled & Canned	2,269
2087 Flavoring Extracts & Flavoring Syrups, nec	614
2091 Canned & Cured Seafoods	347
2092 Fish, Fresh or Frozen	751
2095 Coffee, Roasted	214
2097 Ice	1,040
2098 Macaroni & Spaghetti	356
2099 Food Preparations, nec	2,923
21 **Tobacco Manufacturers**	264
2111 Cigarettes	59
2121 Cigars	91
2131 Tobacco, Chewing & Smoking	69
2141 Tobacco Stemming & Redrying	45
22 **Textile Mill Products**	12,920
2211 Weaving Mills, Cotton	1,306
2221 Weaving Mills, Synthetics	1,059
2231 Weaving & Finishing Mills, Wool	314
2241 Fabric Mills	667
2251 Women's Hosiery	356
2252 Hosiery, nec	563
2253 Knit Outerwear Mills	1,909
2254 Knit Underwear Mills	141
2257 Circle Knit Fabric Mills	263
2258 Warp Knit Fabric Mills	216
2259 Knitting Mills, nec	115
2261 Finishing Plants, Cottons	1,264
2262 Finishing Plants, Synthetics	758
2269 Finishing Plants, Misc.	308
2271 Carpets, Rugs—Woven	260
2272 Carpets, Rugs—Tufted	590
2279 Carpets, Rugs, nec	132
2281 Yarn Mills, Except Wool	443
2282 Mills, Throwing & Winding	145
2283 Mills, Wool Yarn	188
2284 Mills, Thread	138
2291 Felt Goods, Misc.	134
2292 Lace Goods	121
2293 Upholstery Fillings & Padding	141
2294 Textile Waste, Processed	141

SIC DESCRIPTION	NO. OF ESTAB.
2295 Fabrics, Coated Not Rubberized	343
2296 Tire Cord, Fabric	42
2297 Fabrics, Nonwoven	111
2298 Cordage & Twine	360
2299 Textile Goods, nec	392
23 Apparel & Other Textile Products	**40,462**
2311 Men's & Boys' Suits	975
2321 Men's & Boys' Nightwear	1,446
2322 Men's & Boys' Underwear	150
2323 Men's & Boys' Neckwear	348
2327 Men's & Boys' Trousers	796
2328 Men's & Boys' Work Clothing	685
2329 Men's & Boys' Clothing, nec	2,035
2331 Women's & Misses' Blouses	3,258
2335 Women's & Misses' Dresses	4,627
2337 Women's & Misses' Suits	2,934
2339 Women's & Misses' Outerwear, nec	4,963
2341 Women's & Children's Underwear	963
2342 Corsets & Garments	215
2351 Millinery	179
2352 Hats & Caps	482
2361 Children's Dresses	1,015
2363 Children's Coats	175
2369 Children's Outerwear, nec	746
2371 Fur Coats	676
2381 Gloves, Dress & Work	154
2384 Robes & Dress Gowns	246
2385 Waterproof Garments	277
2386 Leather-Lined Cloths	387
2387 Apparel Belts	702
2389 Apparel & Accessories, nec	607
2391 Curtains, Draperies	2,494
2392 Housefurnishings	2,263
2393 Textile Bags	466
2394 Canvas Products	2,049
2395 Pleating & Stitching	954
2396 Apparel Findings	1,322
2397 Schiffli Machine Embroideries	309
2399 Fabricated Textile Products, nec	1,564
24 Lumber & Wood Products	**40,388**
2411 Logging Camps & Contractors	6,462
2421 Sawmills & Planing Mills, General	5,778
2426 Hardwood Dimension Flooring	1,133
2429 Special Product Sawmills, nec	426
2431 Millwork	5,316
2434 Wood Kitchen Cabinets	7,056
2435 Hardwood Veneer & Plywood	492
2436 Softwood Veneer Plywood	243
2439 Structural Wood, nec	1,211
2441 Boxes, Wood	678
2448 Wood Pallets & Skids	2,300
2449 Wood Containers, nec	600

SIC DESCRIPTION	NO. OF ESTAB.
2451 Mobile Homes	652
2452 Wood Buildings, Prefabricated	1,261
2491 Wood Preserving	674
2492 Particleboard	71
2499 Wood Products, nec	6,035
25 Furniture & Fixtures	**21,378**
2511 Wood Household Furniture	5,320
2512 Furniture, Household, Upholstered	3,001
2514 Metal Household Furniture	837
2515 Mattresses & Bedsprings	1,302
2517 Wooden TV & Radio Cabinets	171
2519 Household Furniture, nec	812
2521 Wood Office Furniture	1,893
2522 Metal Office Furniture	586
2531 Furniture for Public Buildings	718
2541 Wood Partitions & Fixtures	3,121
2542 Metal Partitions & Fixtures	1,300
2591 Venetian Blinds, Shades	1,108
2599 Furniture & Fixtures, nec	1,209
26 Paper & Allied Products	**10,011**
2611 Pulp Mills	208
2621 Paper Mills Except Building Paper Mills	785
2631 Paperboard Mills	411
2641 Paper Coating & Glazing	1,072
2642 Envelopes	435
2643 Bags, Except Textile Bags	700
2645 Die Cut Paper, Board	644
2646 Pulp Goods, Pressure Molded	65
2647 Sanitary Paper Products	186
2648 Stationery Products	311
2649 Converted Paper Products	1,256
2651 Boxes, Folding Paperboard	783
2652 Boxes, Setup Paperboard	323
2653 Boxes, Corrugated & Solid Fiber	1,863
2654 Sanitary Food Containers	193
2655 Fiber Cans, Drums, etc.	419
2661 Building Paper & Building Board Mills	357
27 Printing & Publishing	**91,600**
2711 Newspapers	10,148
2721 Periodicals	6,284
2731 Book Publishing	5,954
2732 Book Printing	599
2741 Publishing, Misc.	3,974
2751 Commercial Letterpress Printing	18,027
2752 Commercial Lithographic Printing	35,381
2753 Engraving & Plate Printing	1,308
2754 Commercial Printing, Gravure	649
2761 Manifold Business Forms	847
2771 Greeting Card Publishing	452
2782 Loose Leaf Binders & Blank Books	747
2789 Bookbinding & Related Work	1,349
2791 Typesetting	4,966

SIC DESCRIPTION	NO. OF ESTAB.
2793 Photoengraving	381
2794 Electrotyping & Stereotyping	32
2795 Lithographic Platemaking Services	502
28 Chemicals & Allied Products	24,395
2812 Alkalies, Chlorine	156
2813 Industrial Gases	630
2816 Inorganic Pigments	242
2819 Industrial Inorganic Chemicals, nec	2,195
2821 Plastics Material	1,464
2822 Synthetic Rubber	316
2823 Cellulosic Man-made Fibers	68
2824 Organic Fibers	165
2831 Biological Products	481
2833 Medicinal, Botanical Products	571
2834 Pharmaceutical Preparations	1,658
2841 Soap, Other Detergent	919
2842 Polishing, Cleaning & Sanitation Goods	2,296
2843 Surface Active Agents	228
2844 Toilet Preparations	1,945
2851 Paints & Allied Products	2,148
2861 Gum & Wood Chemicals	198
2865 Cyclic Crudes & Intermediates	341
2869 Industrial Organic Chemicals, nec	1,305
2873 Fertilizers, Nitrogenous	612
2874 Fertilizers, Phosphatic	261
2875 Fertilizers, Mixing	657
2879 Agricultural Chemicals, nec	877
2891 Adhesives & Sealants	1,184
2892 Explosives	171
2893 Printing Ink	614
2895 Carbon Black	53
2899 Chemical Preparations, nec	2,640
29 Petroleum & Coal Products	3,830
2911 Petroleum Refining	1,229
2951 Paving Mixtures & Blocks	1,245
2952 Asphalt Felts & Coatings	419
2992 Lubricating Oils & Greases	835
2999 Petroleum & Coal Products, nec	102
30 Rubber & Misc. Plastics Products	19,724
3011 Tires, Inner Tubes	259
3021 Rubber/Plastic Footwear	104
3031 Reclaimed Rubber	65
3041 Rubber/Plastic Hose	341
3069 Rubber Products, Fabricated, nec	2,265
3079 Plastic Products, Misc.	16,690
31 Leather & Leather Products	5,653
3111 Leather Tanning & Finishing	574
3131 Footwear, Boot & Shoe Cut Stock	223
3142 House Slippers	75
3143 Men's Shoes Except Athletic	443
3144 Ladies' Shoes Except Athletic	477
3149 Footwear Except Rubber, nec	365

SIC DESCRIPTION	NO. OF ESTAB.
3151 Leather Gloves & Mittens	129
3161 Luggage	588
3171 Women's Handbags	805
3172 Leather Goods, Personal, nec	751
3199 Leather Goods, nec	1,223
32 Stone, Clay & Glass Products	24,604
3211 Glass, Flat	425
3221 Glass Containers	204
3229 Glass, Glassware, Pressed or Blown, nec	849
3231 Glass Products, Made of Purchased Glass	2,427
3241 Cement Hydraulic	328
3251 Brick & Structural Clay Tile	413
3253 Ceramic Wall & Floor Tile	258
3255 Clay Refractories	249
3259 Structural Clay Products, nec	128
3261 Vitreous Plumbing Fixtures	171
3262 Vitreous China Food Utensils	88
3263 Food Utensils, Earthenware	46
3264 Porcelain Electrical Supplies	143
3269 Pottery Products, nec	1,390
3271 Concrete Block & Brick	1,591
3272 Concrete Products, nec	4,713
3273 Concrete, Ready-mixed	5,812
3274 Lime	169
3275 Gypsum Products	207
3281 Cut Stone & Stone Products	1,529
3291 Abrasive Products	530
3292 Asbestos Products	276
3293 Gaskets, Packing & Sealing Devices	738
3295 Minerals & Earths, Ground or Treated	542
3296 Mineral Wool	309
3297 Refractories, Nonclay	215
3299 Mineral Products, Nonmetallic, nec	854
33 Primary Metal Industries	12,769
3312 Blast Furnaces, Steel Mills	1,302
3313 Electrometallurgical Products	88
3315 Steel Wire & Related Products	441
3316 Steel—Sheet, Strip & Bar	413
3317 Steel Pipe, Tubes	376
3321 Foundries, Gray Iron	1,129
3322 Foundries, Malleable Iron	127
3324 Steel Investment Foundry	135
3325 Steel Foundries, nec	526
3331 Copper, Primary	48
3332 Lead, Primary	36
3333 Zinc, Primary	43
3334 Aluminum, Primary	123
3339 Metals, Nonferrous Primary Smelting & Refining, nec	345
3341 Metals, Nonferrous, Secondary	817
3351 Copper Rolling, Drawing & Extruding	288
3353 Aluminum Sheet Plate & Foil	132
3354 Aluminum Extruded Products	299

SIC DESCRIPTION	NO. OF ESTAB.
3355 Aluminum Rolling & Drawing, nec	101
3356 Metal, Nonferrous, Rolling, Drawing, nec	373
3357 Wire, Nonferrous, Drawing & Insulating of, Misc.	602
3361 Aluminum Castings	1,664
3362 Brass, Bronze, Copper Castings	1,081
3369 Foundries, Nonferrous, nec	960
3398 Metal Heat Treating	786
3399 Metal Products, Primary, nec	533
34 Fabricated Metal Products	56,636
3411 Metal Cans	550
3412 Metal Drums & Pails	240
3421 Cutlery	277
3423 Hand & Edge Tools, Except Machine Tools & Hand Saws	1,403
3425 Hand Saws & Saw Blades	264
3429 Hardware, nec	2,566
3431 Metal Sanitary Ware	345
3432 Plumbing Fixtures & Brass Goods	404
3433 Heating Equipment Except Electrical	1,592
3442 Metal Doors, Sash, Trim	3,509
3443 Fabricated Plate Work	3,203
3444 Steel Metal Work	5,760
3446 Architectural & Ornamental Metal Work	2,759
3448 Metal Buildings, Prefabricated	1,209
3449 Metal Work, Misc.	507
3451 Screw Machine Products	2,138
3452 Bolts, Nuts, Screws, Rivets & Washers	1,238
3462 Iron & Steel Forgings	734
3463 Forgings, Nonferrous	123
3465 Automotive Stampings	815
3466 Crowns & Closures	59
3469 Metal Stampings, nec	4,377
3471 Plating & Polishing	4,261
3479 Metal Coating & Allied Services	3,073
3482 Ammunition, Small Arms	221
3483 Ammunition, Except for Small Arms, nec	127
3484 Weapons, Small Firearms	322
3489 Ordnance & Accessories, nec	135
3493 Steel Springs	353
3494 Valves, Pipe Fittings	1,928
3495 Wire Springs	386
3496 Fabricated Wire Products, Misc.	2,016
3497 Metal Foil, Leaf	84
3498 Fabricated Pipe & Fittings	1,015
3499 Fabricated Metal Products, nec	3,597
35 Machinery, Except Electrical	90,709
3511 Steam Engines, Turbines	269
3519 Internal Combustion Engines, nec	458
3523 Farm Machinery & Equipment	3,372
3524 Lawn & Garden Equipment	312
3531 Construction Machinery	1,765
3532 Mining Machinery	719
3533 Oil Field Machinery	1,857

SIC DESCRIPTION	NO. OF ESTAB.
3534 Elevator, Moving Stairways	314
3535 Conveyors & Conveying Equipment	1,267
3536 Hoists, Cranes, Monorail Systems	551
3537 Trucks & Tractors, Industrial	995
3541 Machine Tools (Metal Cut)	2,391
3542 Machine Tools, Metal Forming	1,105
3544 Special Dies, Tools	10,033
3545 Machine Tool Accessories	3,406
3546 Power Driven Hand Tool	459
3547 Rolling Mill Machinery	153
3549 Metalworking Machinery, nec	782
3551 Food Products Machinery	1,611
3552 Textile Machinery	918
3553 Woodworking Machinery	547
3554 Paper Industries Machinery	418
3555 Printing Trades Machinery	1,122
3559 Machinery, Special Industries, nec	3,286
3561 Pumps & Pumping Equipment	1,293
3562 Ball & Roller Bearings	326
3563 Air & Gas Compressors	548
3564 Blowers & Exhaust & Ventilation Fans	1,097
3565 Industrial Patterns	1,164
3566 Speed Gear Changers	412
3567 Industrial Furnaces & Ovens	814
3568 Power Transmission Equipment, nec	344
3569 Industrial Machinery & Equipment, nec	3,449
3572 Typewriters	73
3573 Electronic Computing Equipment	4,186
3574 Calculating & Accounting Machines	138
3576 Scales & Balances	233
3579 Office Machines, nec	524
3581 Automatic Merchandising Machines	215
3582 Commercial Laundry Equipment	159
3585 Refrigeration & Heating Equipment	1,653
3586 Measuring & Dispensing Pumps	105
3589 Machines, Service Industry, nec	1,658
3592 Carburetors, Pistons, Piston Rings & Valves	277
3599 Machinery, Except Electrical, nec	33,931
36 Electric & Electronic Equipment	33,186
3612 Transformers	755
3613 Switchgear & Switchboard Apparatus	1,263
3621 Motors & Generators	1,053
3622 Industrial Controls	1,702
3623 Welding Apparatus	362
3624 Carbon & Graphite Products	130
3629 Electrical Industrial Apparatus, nec	465
3631 Household Cooking Equipment	237
3632 Refrigerators & Home Freezers	117
3633 Laundry Equipment, Household	59
3634 Electric Housewares & Fans	588
3635 Vacuum Cleaners, Household	76
3636 Sewing Machines	148

SIC DESCRIPTION	NO. OF ESTAB.
3639 Household Appliances, nec	186
3641 Electric Lamps	520
3643 Current Carrying Wiring Devices	821
3644 Wiring Devices, Non-Current Carrying	346
3645 Lighting Fixtures, Residential	1,171
3646 Lighting Fixtures, Commercial	556
3647 Vehicular Lighting Equipment	173
3648 Lighting Equipment, nec	417
3651 Radio & Television Receiving Sets	1,157
3652 Phonograph Records	1,592
3661 Telephone & Telegraph Apparatus	1,081
3662 Radio & Television Communication Equipment	5,312
3671 Electron Tubes, Radio & TV Receiving Types	52
3672 Cathode Ray Picture Tubes (TV)	71
3673 Electron Tubes & Transmitting, Industrial	113
3674 Semiconductors & Related Devices	2,631
3675 Electronic Capacitors	173
3676 Electronic Resistors	108
3677 Electronic Coils, Transformers & Other Inductors	464
3678 Electronic Connectors	184
3679 Electronic Components, nec	6,221
3691 Batteries, Storage	262
3692 Batteries, Primary: Dry & Wet	163
3693 X-Ray Apparatus & Tubes	505
3694 Engines, Electrical Equipment for	848
3699 Electric Equipment, nec	1,104
37 Transportation Equipment	**18,052**
3711 Motor Vehicle Bodies	1,181
3713 Truck & Bus Bodies	1,387
3714 Motor Vehicle Parts & Accessories	4,498
3715 Truck Trailers	824
3721 Aircraft	373
3724 Aircraft Engines & Engine Parts	577
3728 Aircraft Equipment, nec	1,846
3731 Ship Building & Repairing	967
3732 Boat Building & Repairing	2,981
3743 Railroad Equipment	345
3751 Motorcycles, Bicycle Parts	659
3761 Guided Missiles & Space Vehicles	80
3764 Guided Missiles, Space Vehicle Propulsion Units	52
3769 Space Vehicle Equipment, nec	84
3792 Travel Trailers & Campers	1,232
3795 Tanks & Tank Components	38
3799 Transportation Equipment, nec	928
38 Instrument & Related Products	**18,948**
3811 Engineering Laboratory Scientific & Related Equipment	1,779
3822 Automatic Temperature Controls	925
3823 Process Control Instruments	2,567
3824 Fluid Meters & Counting Devices	376
3825 Instruments for Measuring Electricity	1,743
3829 Measuring & Controlling Devices, nec	1,384
3832 Eye Instruments & Lenses	945

SIC	DESCRIPTION	NO. OF ESTAB.
3841	Surgical & Medical Instruments	1,959
3842	Surgical Appliances & Supplies	2,494
3843	Dental Equipment & Supplies	1,087
3851	Ophthalmic Goods	1,506
3861	Photographic Equipment & Supplies	1,589
3873	Watches/Watchcases & Clocks	594
39	**Misc. Manufacturing Industries**	34,747
3911	Jewelry, Precious Metals	5,244
3914	Silverware & Plated Ware	529
3915	Jewelers' Material & Lapidary	813
3931	Musical Instruments and Parts	844
3942	Dolls	724
3944	Games/Toys & Children's Vehicles	2,041
3949	Athletic & Sporting Goods, nec	4,311
3951	Pens & Mechanical Pencils	232
3952	Lead Pencils & Artists' Goods	390
3953	Marking Devices	1,253
3955	Carbon Paper & Inked Ribbons	227
3961	Jewelry, Costume	1,913
3962	Flowers, Artificial	480
3963	Buttons	189
3964	Needles, Pins & Fasteners	491
3991	Brooms & Brushes	548
3993	Signs & Advertising Displays	5,820
3995	Burial Caskets	358
3996	Floor Coverings, Hard Surface	50
3999	Manufacturing Industries, nec	8,290
	TRANSPORTATION, COMMUNICATION & PUBLIC	
	UTILITIES	240,673
40	**Railroad Transportation**	1,247
4011	Railroads, Line-Haul Operating	965
4013	Switching & Terminal Establishments	264
4041	Railway Express Services	18
41	**Local & Interurban Passenger Transit**	14,674
4111	Local & Suburban Transportation	1,068
4119	Passenger Transportation, Local, nec	5,304
4121	Taxicabs	2,761
4131	Intercity Highway Transportation	708
4141	Passenger Charter Services	948
4142	Charter Service, Except Local	1,107
4151	School Buses	2,411
4171	Bus Terminal Services	281
4172	Bus Service Facilities	86
42	**Trucking & Warehousing**	125,356
4212	Trucking Without Storage, Local	54,483
4213	Trucking, Except Local	42,514
4214	Trucking With Storage, Local	6,810
4221	Farm Product Warehousing & Storage	2,815
4222	Refrigerated Warehousing	2,722
4224	Warehousing, Household Goods	1,337
4225	Warehousing & Storage, General	10,998
4226	Warehousing & Storage, nec	2,386

SIC DESCRIPTION	NO. OF ESTAB.
4231 Terminal Facilities	1,291
43 U.S. Postal Service	325
4311 U.S. Postal Service	325
44 Water Transportation	12,631
4411 Foreign Deep Sea Transportation	597
4421 Transportation, Noncontiguous Deep Sea	142
4422 Coastwise Transportation	197
4423 Intercoastal Transportation	80
4431 Great Lakes Transportation	49
4441 Transportation on Rivers & Canals	438
4452 Ferries	68
4453 Lighterage	51
4454 Towing & Tugboat Services	1,217
4459 Water Transportation, Local, nec	484
4463 Marine Cargo Handling	1,200
4464 Canal Operation	15
4469 Water Transportation Services, nec	8,093
45 Transportation by Air	11,862
4511 Air Transportation, Certified Carriers	2,360
4521 Air Transportation, Non-Certified Carriers	3,541
4582 Airports & Flying Fields	5,458
4583 Airport Terminal Services	503
46 Pipe Lines, Except Natural Gas	713
4612 Crude Petroleum Pipe Lines	374
4613 Refined Petroleum Pipe Lines	283
4619 Pipe Lines, nec	56
47 Transportation Services	33,551
4712 Freight Forwarding	5,870
4722 Passenger Transportation Arrangement	19,890
4723 Freight & Cargo Transportation	5,891
4742 Railroad Car Rental With Services	142
4743 Railroad Car Rental Without Services	88
4782 Inspection & Weighing Services	263
4783 Packing & Crating	781
4784 Fixed Facilities for Vehicles, nec	67
4789 Transportation Services, nec	559
48 Communication	20,988
4811 Telephone Communications	4,667
4821 Telegraph Communications	515
4832 Radio Broadcasting	7,121
4833 Television Broadcasting	2,139
4899 Communication Services, nec	6,546
49 Electric, Gas & Sanitary Services	19,326
4911 Electric Services	3,358
4922 Natural Gas Transmission	864
4923 Natural Gas Transmission & Distribution	632
4924 Natural Gas Distribution	1,008
4925 Petroleum Gas Production and/or Distribution	274
4931 Electric & Other Services Combined	457
4932 Gas & Other Services Combined	142
4939 Utilities, nec	30
4941 Water Supply	3,506

SIC DESCRIPTION	NO. OF ESTAB.
4952 Sewerage Systems	1,147
4953 Refuse Systems	4,473
4959 Sanitary Services, nec	2,761
4961 Steam Supply	142
4971 Irrigation Systems	532
WHOLESALE TRADE	761,009
50 Wholesale Trade—Durable Goods	480,596
5012 Automobiles & Other Motor Vehicles	9,998
5013 Automotive Equipment	53,208
5014 Tires & Tubes	10,496
5021 Furniture	12,743
5023 Home Furnishings	15,587
5031 Lumber, Plywood, Millwork	13,814
5039 Construction Materials, nec	22,755
5041 Sporting & Amusement Goods	10,329
5042 Toys & Hobby Goods Supply	3,971
5043 Photo Equipment & Supply	2,685
5051 Metal Service Centers & Offices	12,713
5052 Coal/Minerals & Ores	1,678
5063 Electrical Apparatus & Equipment	25,272
5064 Electrical Appliances, Television & Radio	9,002
5065 Electronic Parts & Equipment	17,181
5072 Hardware	12,762
5074 Plumbing & Hydronic Supplies	14,823
5075 Warm Air Heating, Air Conditioning	6,622
5078 Refrigeration Equipment & Supplies	3,376
5081 Commercial Machines & Equipment	38,025
5082 Construction & Mining Machinery	8,420
5083 Farm Machinery & Equipment	22,182
5084 Industrial Machinery & Equipment	48,339
5085 Industrial Supplies	18,863
5086 Professional Equipment & Supplies	16,888
5087 Service Establishment Equipment	14,600
5088 Transportation Equipment & Supplies	5,422
5093 Scrap & Waste Material	8,949
5094 Jewelry & Watches	12,571
5099 Durable Goods, nec	27,322
51 Wholesale Trade—Nondurable Goods	280,413
5111 Printing & Writing Paper	2,070
5112 Stationery & Supply	12,244
5113 Industrial & Personal Service Paper	7,293
5122 Drugs & Proprietaries	7,594
5133 Piece Goods	6,154
5134 Notions & Dry Goods	2,736
5136 Men's Clothing & Furnishings	8,902
5137 Women's & Children's Clothing	13,838
5139 Footwear	2,499
5141 Groceries, General Line	12,696
5142 Frozen Foods	3,513
5143 Dairy Products	4,863
5144 Poultry & Its Products	2,668
5145 Confectionery	7,083

SIC DESCRIPTION	NO. OF ESTAB.
5146 Fish & Seafoods	5,369
5147 Meat & Meat Products	8,246
5148 Fresh Fruits & Vegetables	7,337
5149 Groceries & Its Products, nec	13,281
5152 Cotton	593
5153 Grain	9,549
5154 Livestock	3,574
5159 Farm Product Raw Materials, nec	2,534
5161 Chemicals & Allied Products	15,404
5171 Petroleum Bulk Stations & Terminals	11,861
5172 Petroleum Products, nec	13,867
5181 Beer & Ale	5,050
5182 Wines & Distilled Beverages	3,308
5191 Farm Supplies	30,684
5194 Tobacco & Its Products	2,582
5198 Paints, Varnishes & Supplies	5,985
5199 Nondurable Goods, nec	47,036
RETAIL TRADE	1,887,151
52 Bldg. Materials & Garden Supplies	140,732
5211 Lumber & Building Materials	40,945
5231 Paint, Glass & Wallpaper Stores	21,628
5251 Hardware Stores	42,458
5261 Nurseries, Lawn & Garden Supply Stores	26,454
5271 Mobile Home Dealers	9,247
53 General Merchandise Stores	47,787
5311 Department Stores	10,085
5331 Variety Stores	9,986
5399 General Merchandise Stores	27,716
54 Food Stores	180,170
5411 Grocery Stores	124,961
5422 Freezer & Food Plan Provisions	734
5423 Meat & Seafood (Fish) Markets	14,563
5431 Fruit & Vegetable Markets	4,518
5441 Candy, Nut & Confectionery Stores	7,545
5451 Dairy Products Stores	4,361
5462 Bakeries, Baking & Selling	13,913
5463 Bakeries, Selling Only	901
5499 Food Stores, Misc.	8,674
55 Auto Dealers & Service Stations	258,621
5511 Car Dealers, New & Used	31,519
5521 Car Dealers, Used Only	25,032
5531 Auto & Home Supply Stores	65,434
5541 Gasoline Service Stations	105,249
5551 Boat Dealers	11,874
5561 Recreational & Utility Trailer Dealers	5,631
5571 Motorcycle Dealers	7,725
5599 Automotive Dealers, nec	6,157
56 Apparel & Accessory Stores	178,941
5611 Men's & Boys' Clothing & Furnishings	25,232
5621 Women's Ready-to-wear Stores	58,362
5631 Women's Accessory & Specialty Stores	13,087
5641 Children's & Infants' Wear Stores	12,685

SIC DESCRIPTION	NO. OF ESTAB.
5651 Family Clothing Stores	13,583
5661 Shoe Stores	29,749
5681 Furrier & Fur Shops	1,320
5699 Apparel & Accessories, Misc.	24,923
57 Furniture & Home Furnishings Stores	216,997
5712 Furniture Stores	56,929
5713 Floor Covering Stores	31,834
5714 Drapery & Upholstery Stores	13,052
5719 Home Furnishing Stores	25,750
5722 Household Appliance Stores	35,937
5732 Radio & Television Stores	38,852
5733 Music Stores	14,643
58 Eating & Drinking Places	321,717
5812 Restaurants, Diners, Eating Places	219,310
5813 Bars, Night Clubs (Drinking Places)	102,407
59 Miscellaneous Retail	542,186
5912 Drug & Proprietary Stores	43,659
5921 Liquor Stores	47,170
5931 Used Merchandise Stores	36,277
5941 Sporting Goods & Bicycle Stores	55,735
5942 Book Stores	12,824
5943 Stationery Stores	15,181
5944 Jewelry Stores	33,950
5945 Hobby, Toy & Game Shops	12,530
5946 Photographic Supply Stores	6,693
5947 Gift & Novelty Shops	72,542
5948 Luggage & Leather Goods Stores	3,204
5949 Sewing, Needlework & Piece Goods Stores	16,838
5961 Mail Order Houses	10,674
5962 Vending Machine, Machine Operators	8,366
5963 Direct Selling Companies	5,668
5982 Fuel & Ice Dealers, nec	2,105
5983 Fuel Oil Dealers	10,225
5984 Bottle Gas Dealers (Liquified Petroleum)	6,580
5992 Florists	30,575
5993 Cigar Stores & Stands	3,670
5994 News Dealers & Newsstands	3,062
5999 Miscellaneous Retail Store, nec	104,658
FINANCE, INSURANCE & REAL ESTATE	566,295
60 Banking	52,680
6000 Banks	400
6011 Federal Reserve Banks	325
6022 State Banks, Members of Federal Reserve System, Insured	11,039
6023 State Banks, Not Members of Federal Reserve System, Insured	14,020
6024 State Banks, Not Members of Federal Reserve System, Not Insured	349
6025 National Banks, Members of Federal Reserve System, Insured	21,164
6026 National Banks, Not Members of Federal Reserve System, Insured	543

SIC DESCRIPTION	NO. OF ESTAB.
6027 National Banks, Not Members of Federal Reserve System, Not Insured	41
6028 Unicorp Private Banks	47
6032 Mutual Savings Banks, Members of Federal Reserve System, Insured	770
6033 Mutual Savings Banks, Not Members of Federal Reserve System, Insured	1,511
6034 Mutual Savings Banks, Not Members of Federal Reserve System, Not Insured	330
6042 State Nondeposit Trust Companies, Members of Federal Reserve System, Insured & Not Insured	66
6044 State Nondeposit Trust Companies, Not Insured	64
6052 Foreign Exchange Establishments	499
6054 Safe Deposit Company	94
6055 Clearinghouse Associations	43
6056 Corporations, For Banking Abroad	124
6059 Banking Related Services	1,251
61 Credit Agencies Other Than Banks	42,230
6112 Financing Institutions	129
6113 Rediscount for Agriculture	21
6122 Federal Savings & Loan Associations	3,438
6123 State Savings & Loan Associations	2,113
6124 Savings & Loan, Not Insured, Member	247
6125 State Savings & Loan, Not Insured, nec	231
6131 Agricultural Credit Institutions	835
6142 Federal Credit Unions	3,059
6143 State Credit Unions	11,457
6144 Industrial Loan Companies	447
6145 Loan (Small) Lenders, Licensed	3,703
6146 Installment Sales Finance Companies	1,707
6149 Personal Credit Institutions, Misc.	372
6153 Short Term Business Credit Institutions	1,648
6159 Business Credit Institutions, Misc.	3,074
6162 Mortgage Bankers & Loan Correspondents	5,598
6163 Loan Brokers	4,151
62 Security, Commodity Brokers & Svcs.	18,046
6211 Securities Brokers & Dealers	9,842
6221 Commodity Contracts Brokers & Dealers	2,205
6231 Security & Commodity Exchanges	206
6281 Securities or Commodities Service	5,793
63 Insurance Carriers	17,521
6311 Life Insurance	5,415
6321 Accident & Health Insurance	2,347
6324 Hospital & Medical Service Plans	773
6331 Fire, Sea & Casualty Insurance	4,519
6351 Surety Insurance	987
6361 Title Insurance	2,189
6371 Pension, Health & Welfare Funds	946
6399 Insurance Carriers, Misc.	345
64 Insurance Agents, Brokers & Services	119,002
6411 Insurance Agents & Brokers	119,002
65 Real Estate	286,235

SIC DESCRIPTION	NO. OF ESTAB.
6512 Building Operators, Nonresidential	69,080
6513 Apartment Building & Residential Hotel Operators	51,762
6514 Dwelling Operators (Less than 5 Housing Units)	11,435
6515 Residential Mobile Homesites, Operators of	10,006
6517 Railroad Property Lessors	53
6519 Real Property Lessors, nec	5,392
6531 Agents, Managers—Real Estate	94,642
6541 Title Abstract Offices	2,117
6552 Subdividers, Developers, Except Cemeteries	37,676
6553 Cemetery Subdivision & Development	4,072
66 Combined Real Estate, Insurance, etc.	7,999
6611 Real Estate, Insurance, Loans, Law Offices Combined	7,999
67 Holding and Other Investment Offices	22,582
6711 Holding Offices	5,044
6722 Management Investment Offices, Open-end	689
6723 Management Investment Offices, Closed-end	261
6724 Unit Investment Trusts	173
6732 Educational, Religious & Charitable Trusts	1,153
6733 Trusts, Except Educational, Religious & Charitable	1,161
6792 Investors, Oil & Gas Royalties	2,336
6793 Commodity Trading Companies	396
6794 Patent Owners & Lessors	3,070
6799 Investors, Misc.	8,293
SERVICES	1,887,737
70 Hotels & Other Lodging Places	61,923
7011 Hotels/Inns/Tourist Courts	52,369
7021 Rooming/Boarding Houses	1,075
7032 Sports/Amusement Camps	2,430
7033 Trailer Parks for Transients	5,544
7041 Hotels, Lodging, Houses for Membership Organization	505
72 Personal Services	163,813
7211 Laundries, Power, Family & Commercial	3,914
7212 Garment Cleaners & Agents	2,869
7213 Linen Supply	1,834
7214 Diaper Service	205
7215 Coin Laundry/Cleaners	15,091
7216 Dry Cleaning Plants Except Rugs	22,375
7217 Carpet/Upholstery Cleaners	8,453
7218 Industrial/Launderers	1,010
7219 Laundry/Garment Services, nec	4,684
7221 Photographic Studios	10,132
7231 Beauty Shops	43,330
7241 Barber Shops	7,061
7251 Shoe Repair Shops	6,983
7261 Funeral Service	17,171
7299 Personal Services, Misc.	18,701
73 Business Services	382,108
7311 Advertising Agencies	20,410
7312 Advertising Services, Outdoor	1,478
7313 Radio TV Advertising Representatives	900
7319 Advertising, nec	1,856
7321 Credit Reporting & Collection	4,943

SIC DESCRIPTION	NO. OF ESTAB.
7331 Direct Mail Advertising	3,782
7332 Blueprinting & Photocopying	3,657
7333 Commercial Photography/Art	21,186
7339 Steno, Duplicating Services, nec	3,541
7341 Window Cleaning	1,068
7342 Disinfecting & Exterminating	7,785
7349 Janitorial Services, nec	20,409
7351 News Syndicates	450
7361 Employment Agencies	9,125
7362 Temporary Aid Supply Services	3,823
7369 Personnel Supply Services, nec	554
7372 Computer Programming	19,464
7374 Data Processing Services	9,237
7379 Computer Related Services, nec	13,262
7391 Research & Development Laboratories	7,421
7392 Management & Public Relations	74,412
7393 Detective & Protective Services	7,774
7394 Equipment Rental/Leasing	46,998
7395 Photofinishing Labs	7,956
7396 Trading Stamp Services	140
7397 Commercial Testing Laboratories	3,136
7399 Business Services, nec	87,341
75 Auto Repair, Services & Garages	**184,158**
7512 Passenger Car Rental	9,922
7513 Truck Rental & Leasing	8,302
7519 Recreational Vehicle & Trailer Rentals	2,217
7523 Parking Lots	1,109
7525 Parking Structures	721
7531 Top & Body Repair Shops	32,154
7534 Tire Retreading & Repair	4,534
7535 Paint Shops	4,567
7538 Automotive Repair Shops, General	71,994
7539 Automotive Repair Shops, Specialized, nec	29,972
7542 Car Washes	9,529
7549 Automotive Services, Misc.	9,137
76 Miscellaneous Repair Services	**199,254**
7622 Radio & Television Repair	31,289
7623 Refrigeration & Air-conditioning Service & Repair	12,761
7629 Electrical & Electronic Repair Shops, nec	26,394
7631 Watch, Clock & Jewelry Repair	9,934
7641 Reupholstery & Furniture Repair	12,625
7692 Welding Repair	12,465
7694 Armature Rewinding Shops	4,409
7699 Repair Services, nec	89,377
78 Motion Pictures	**22,681**
7813 Motion Picture Production Except Television	4,323
7814 Motion Picture Production for Television	5,256
7819 Motion Picture Production Service	1,934
7823 Motion Picture Film Exchanges	1,030
7824 Film or Tape Distribution for Television	5,516
7829 Motion Picture Distribution Service	330
7832 Motion Picture Theaters	3,278

SIC DESCRIPTION	NO. OF ESTAB.
7833 Drive-in Movies	1,014
79 Amusement & Recreation Services	66,121
7911 Dance Halls & Studios	2,983
7922 Theatrical Producers & Services	4,021
7929 Entertainers	1,717
7932 Billiard & Pool Establishments	1,306
7933 Bowling Alleys	7,738
7941 Sports Clubs & Promoters	962
7948 Race Tracks & Stables	2,102
7992 Golf Courses, Public	3,442
7993 Coin-operated Amusement Devices	5,593
7996 Amusement Parks	717
7997 Membership Sports & Recreation	13,678
7999 Amusement & Recreation Services, nec	21,862
80 Health Services	303,883
8011 Physicians, Offices of	149,180
8021 Dentists, Offices of	79,386
8031 Osteopathic Physicians, Offices of	5,464
8041 Chiropractors, Offices of	16,782
8042 Optometrists, Offices of	5,795
8049 Health Practitioners, nec. Offices of	4,721
8051 Nursing Care Facilities	8,820
8059 Nursing & Personal Care Facilities, nec	5,814
8062 Hospitals, Medical/Surgical	7,319
8063 Hospitals, Psychiatric	981
8069 Specialty Hospitals, Except Psychiatric	835
8071 Medical Laboratories	4,702
8072 Dental Laboratories	5,854
8081 Outpatient Care Facilities	4,881
8091 Health & Allied Services, nec	3,349
81 Legal Services	127,930
8111 Legal Services	127,930
82 Educational Services	144,014
8211 Elementary & Secondary Schools	118,235
8221 Colleges, Universities & Professional Schools	3,315
8222 Junior Colleges & Technical Institutes	1,272
8231 Libraries & Information Centers	2,657
8241 Correspondence Schools	236
8243 Data Processing Schools	505
8244 Business & Secretarial Schools	860
8249 Vocational Schools, nec	3,614
8299 School & Educational Services, nec	13,320
83 Social Services	32,815
8321 Individual & Family Services	6,480
8331 Job Training & Related Services	2,649
8351 Child Day Care Services	9,466
8361 Residential Care	5,887
8399 Social Services, nec	8,333
84 Museums, Botanical, Zoological Gardens	1,821
8411 Museums & Art Galleries	1,667
8421 Botanical & Zoological Gardens	154
86 Membership Organizations	74,480

SIC DESCRIPTION	NO. OF ESTAB.
8611 Business Associations	8,935
8621 Professional Organizations	2,955
8631 Labor Organizations	6,507
8641 Civic & Social Organizations	14,957
8651 Political Organizations	314
8661 Religious Organizations	33,030
8699 Membership Organizations, nec	7,782
89 Miscellaneous Services	122,354
8911 Engineering & Architectural Services	50,825
8922 Noncommercial Research Organization	2,380
8931 Accounting, Auditing & Bookkeeping	57,002
8999 Services, nec	12,147
PUBLIC ADMINISTRATION	73,122
9111 Executive Offices	30,990
9121 Legislative Bodies	4,414
9131 Executives & Legislative Offices Combined	914
9199 General Government, nec	1,427
9211 Courts	230
9221 Police, Enforcement	331
9222 Legal Counsel & Prosecution	201
9223 Correctional Institutions	408
9224 Fire Protection	4,738
9229 Public Order & Safety, nec	150
9311 Public Finance, Taxation, & Monetary Policy	519
9411 Educational Programs, Administration of	10,959
9431 Public Health Programs, Administration of	733
9441 Social Manpower & Income Maintenance Programs, Administration of	474
9451 Veterans Affairs, Except Health & Insurance	106
9511 Air, Water Resource & Solid Waste Management	7,268
9512 Land, Mineral, Wildlife & Forest Conservation	2,943
9531 Housing Programs, Administration of	2,686
9532 Urban Planning & Community Development	524
9611 Economic Programs, Administration of	562
9621 Transportation Programs, Regulation & Administration of	1,301
9631 Communication, Electric, Gas & Other Utilities, Regulation & Administration of	436
9641 Agricultural Marketing & Commodities, Regulation of	192
9651 Regulation, Licensing & Inspection of Misc. Commercial Sectors	254
9711 National Security	798
9721 International Affairs	438

nec—not elsewhere classified

State Development Agencies

Alabama Development Office
c/o State Capitol
Montgomery, AL 36130

Alaska Department of Commerce &
Economic Development
Division of Economic Enterprise
Pouch EE
Juneau, AK 99811

Arizona Office of Economic
Planning & Development
17 West Washington
Phoenix, AZ 85007

Arkansas Industrial Development
Commission
State Capitol
Little Rock, AR 72201

California Department of Economic
& Business Development
Office of Business & Industrial
Development
1120 N St.
Sacramento, CA 95814

Colorado Division of Commerce &
Development
1313 Sherman St., Room 500
Denver, CO 80203

Connecticut Department of
Commerce
210 Washington St.
Hartford, CT 06106

Delaware Department of
Community Affairs & Economic
Development
Division of Economic Development
630 State College Rd.
Dover, DE 19901

Florida Department of Commerce
Division of Economic Development
Collins Building
Tallahassee, FL 32304

Georgia Department of Industry &
Trade
Post Office Box 1776
Atlanta, GA 30301

Hawaii Department of Planning &
Economic Development
Post Office Box 2359
Honolulu, HI 96804

Idaho Division of Tourism &
Industrial Development
State Capitol Building, Room 108
Boise, ID 83720

Illinois Department of Business &
  Economic Development
222 South College St.
Springfield, IL 62706

Indiana Department of Commerce
1350 Consolidated Building
115 North Pennsylvania St.
Indianapolis, IN 46204

Iowa Development Commission
250 Jewett Building
Des Moines, IA 50309

Kansas Department of Economic
  Development
503 Kansas Ave.
Topeka, KS 66603

Kentucky Department of Commerce
Capitol Plaza Office Tower
Frankfort, KY 40601

Louisiana Department of Commerce
  & Industry
Post Office Box 44185
Baton Rouge, LA 70804

Maine State Development Office
Executive Department
State House
Augusta, ME 04333

Maryland Department of Economic
  & Community Development
2525 Riva Rd
Annapolis, MD 21401

Massachusetts Department of
  Commerce & Development
100 Cambridge St.
Boston, MA 02202

Michigan Department of Commerce
Office of Economic Expansion
Post Office Box 30225
Lansing, MI 48909

Minnesota Department of Economic
  Development
480 Cedar St.
St Paul, MN 55101

Mississippi Agricultural & Industrial
  Board

Post Office Box 849
Jackson, MS 39205

Missouri Division of Commerce &
  Industrial Development
Post Office Box 118
Jefferson City, MO 65101

Montana Department of Community
  Affairs
Economic Development Division
Capitol Station
Helena, MT 59601

Nebraska Department of Economic
  Development
Box 94666—State Capitol
Lincoln, NE 68509

Nevada Department of Economic
  Development
Capital Complex
Carson City, NV 89710

New Hampshire Office of Industrial
  Development
Division of Economic Development
Department of Resources &
  Economic Development
Post Office Box 856
Concord, NH 03301

New Jersey Department of Labor &
  Industry
Division of Economic Development
Post Office Box 2766
Trenton, NJ 08625

New Mexico Department of
  Development
113 Washington Ave.
Santa Fe, NM 87503

New York State Department of
  Commerce
99 Washington Ave.
Albany, NY 12245

North Carolina Department of
  Natural and Economic
  Development
Division of Economic Development
Box 27687
Raleigh, NC 27611

North Dakota Business and
Industrial Development
Department
523 East Bismarck Ave.
Bismarck, ND 58505

Ohio Department of Economic and
Community Development
Box 1001
Columbus, OH 43216

Oklahoma Department of Industrial
Development
600 Will Rogers Building
Oklahoma City, OK 73105

Oregon Department of Economic
Development
317 South West Alder St.
Portland, OR 97204

Pennsylvania Department of
Commerce
Division of Research & Planning
632 Health and Welfare Building
Harrisburg, PA 17120

Rhode Island Department of
Economic Development
One Weybosset Hill
Providence, RI 02903

South Carolina State Development
Board
Post Office Box 927
Columbia, SC 29202

South Dakota Department of
Economic & Tourism Development
620 South Cliff
Sioux Falls, SD 57103

Tennessee Department of Economic
& Community Development
1014 Andrew Jackson State Office
Building
Nashville, TN 37219

Texas Industrial Commission
714 Sam Houston State Office
Building
Austin, TX 78711

Utah Department of Development
Services
No. 2 Arrow Press Square, Suite 200
165 South West Temple
Salt Lake City, UT 84101

Vermont Agency of Development &
Community Affairs
Economic Development Department
Pavilion Office Building
Montpelier, VT 05602

Virginia Division of Industrial
Development
1010 State Office Building
Richmond, VA 23219

Washington State Department of
Commerce & Economic
Development
101 General Administration
Building
Olympia, WA 98504

West Virginia Department of
Commerce
Industrial Development Division
1900 Washington St. East
Charleston, WV 25305

Wisconsin Department of Business
Development
123 West Washington Ave.
Madison, WI 53702

Wyoming Department of Economic
Planning & Development
Barrett Building, Third Floor
Cheyenne, WY 82002

Small Business Administration Field Offices

Alabama
908 South 20th St.
Birmingham AL 35205
205/254-1344

Alaska
Federal Building
701 C St. Box 67
Anchorage, AK 99513
907/217-4022

Box 14
101 12th Ave.
Fairbanks, AK 99701
907/452-0211

Arizona
3030 North Central Ave.
Suite 1201
Phoenix, AZ 85012
602/241-2200

301 West Congress St.
Federal Building Room 3V
Tucson, AZ 85701
602/792-6715

Arkansas
PO Box 1401
Little Rock, AK 72203
501/378-5871

California
1229 N St.
Fresno, CA 93712
209/487-5189

350 S. Figueroa St.
6th Floor
Los Angeles, CA 90071
213/688-2956

1515 Clay St.
Oakland CA 94612
414/273-7790

2800 Cottage Way
Room W2535
Sacramento, CA 95825
916/484-4726

*880 Front St.
Room 4-S-33
San Diego, CA 92188
714/293-5440

*450 Golden Gate Ave.
PO Box 36044
San Francisco, CA 94102
415/556-7487

*Regional Office

211 Main St.
4th Floor
San Francisco, CA 94105
415/556-2820

Fidelity Federal Building
2700 North Main St.
Santa Ana, CA 92701
714/547-5089

Colorado
*Executive Tower Building
1405 Curtis St.
22nd Floor
Denver, CO 80202
303/837-5763

721 19th St.
Room 407
Denver, CO 80202
303/837-2607

Connecticut
One Hartford Square W.
Hartford, CT 06106
603/224-4041

Delaware
844 King Street
Room 5207
Lockbox 16
Wilmington, DE 19801
302/573-6294

District of Columbia
111 18th St., NW
Sixth Floor
Washington, DC 20417
202/634-1818

Florida
400 West Bay St.
Room 261
PO Box 35067
Jacksonville, FL 32202
904/791-3782

2222 Ponce De Leon Blvd.
5th Floor
Coral Gables, FL 33134
305/350-5521

Regional Office

700 Twiggs St.
Suite 607
Tampa, FL 33602
813/228-2594

701 Clematis St.
Room 229
West Palm Beach FL 33402
305/659-7533

Georgia
*1375 Peachtree St. NW
5th Floor
Atlanta, GA 30309
404/881-4943

1720 Peachtree St. NW
6th Floor
Atlanta, GA 30309
404/881-4325

Federal Building
52 North Main St.
Statesboro, GA 30458
912/489-8719

Guam
Pacific Daily News Building
Room 508, Martyr and Chara Sts.
Agena, GU 96910
671/477-8420

Hawaii
300 Ala Moana
Room 2213
PO Box 50207
Honolulu, HI 96850
808/546-8950

Idaho
1005 Main St., 2nd Floor
Boise, ID 83702
208/334-1096

Illinois
219 South Dearborn St.
Room 438
Chicago, IL 60604
312/353-4528

Illinois National Bank Bldg.
1 North Old State
Capital Plaza
Springfield, IL 62701

217/492-4416

Indiana
501 E. Monroe St.
Suite 120
South Bend, IN 46601
219/232-8163

New Federal Building
5th Floor
575 N. Pennsylvania St.
Indianapolis, IN 46204
317/269-7272

Iowa
210 Walnut St.
Des Moines, IA 50309
515/284-4422
 373 Collins Rd NE
Cedar Rapids, IA 52402
319/399-2571

Kansas
Main Place Bldg.
110 East Waterman St.
Wichita, KA 67202
316/267-6311

Kentucky
Federal Office Bldg.
PO Box 3517
Room 188
Louisville, KY 40201
502/582-5971

Louisiana
Ford-Fish Bldg.
1661 Canal St.
2nd Floor
New Orleans, LA 70112
504/589-6685

500 Fannin Street
Federal Bldg. & Courthouse, Room
 5 BO4
Shreveport, LA 71101
318/226-5196

Maine
40 Western Ave.
Room 512
Augusta, ME 04330
207/622-6171

Maryland
8600 LaSalle Rd.
Room 630
Towson, MD 21204
301/962-4392

Massachusetts
*60 Batterymarch St.
10th Floor
Boston, MA 02110
617/223-2100

150 Causeway St.
10th Floor
Boston, MA 02114
617/223-2100

302 High Street
4th Floor
Holyoke, MA 01040
413/536-8770

Michigan
477 Michigan Ave.
McNamara Bldg.
Room 515
Detroit, MI 48226
313/226-6000

Don H. Bottum University Ctr.
540 W. Kaye Ave.
Marquette, MI 49885
906/225-1108

Minnesota
610 C-Butler Square
100 North 6th St.
Minneapolis, MN 55403
612/725-2928

Mississippi
Gulf National Life Insurance Bldg.
111 Fred Haise Blvd.
2nd Floor
Biloxi, MS 39530
601/435-3676

100 West Capitol St.
New Federal Bldg.
Suite 322
Jackson, MS 30201

Regional Office

601/969-4371

Missouri
*911 Walnut St.
23rd Floor
Kansas City, MO 64106
816/374-3316

1150 Grand Ave.
5th Floor
Kansas City, MO 64106
816/374-5557

815 Olive St.
Room 242
St. Louis, MO 63101
314/425-6600

731 North Main
Sikeston, MO 63801
314/471-0223

309 North Jefferson
Springfield, MO 65806
417/864-7670

Montana
301 South Park Ave
Room 528,
Drawer 10054
Helena, MT 59601
406/446-5381

Nebraska
Empire State Building
19th & Farnum St.
Omaha, NE 68102
402/221-4691

New Jersey
1800 East Davis St.
Camden, NJ 08104
609/757-5183

970 Broad St.
Room 1635
Newark, NJ 07102
201/645-3683

New Mexico
Patio Plaza Building
5000 Marble Ave. NE
Albuquerque, NM 87110
505/766-3430

New York
99 Washington Ave.
Room 921
Albany, NY 12210
518/472-6300

111 West Huron St.
Room 1311
Buffalo, NY 14202
716/846-4301

180 Clemens Center Pkwy.
Room 412
Elmira, NY 14901
607/733-4686

35 Pinelaw Rd
Room 102 E.
Melville, NY 11747
515/454-0764

*26 Federal Plaza
Room 29-118
New York, NY 10007
212/264-7772

26 Federal Plaza
Room 3100
New York, NY 10007
212/264-1766

100 State St.
Room 601
Rochester, NY 14614
716/263-6700

100 South Clinton St.
Room 1073
Federal Bldg.
Syracuse, NY 13260
315/423-5382

North Carolina
230 S. Tryon St.
Suite 700
Charlotte, NC 28202
704/371-6111

215 South Evans St.
Room 206
Greenville, NC 27834
919/752-3798

Regional Office

North Dakota
PO Box 3086
Fargo, ND 58102
701/237-5131

Ohio
1240 East 9th St.
Room 317
AJA Federal Bldg.
Cleveland, OH 44199
216/522-4194

85 Marconi Boulevard
Columbus, OH 43215
614/469-6860

550 Main St.
Room 5028
Cincinnati, OH 45202
513/684-2814

Oklahoma
200 NW 5th St.
Suite 670
Oklahoma City, OK 73102
405/231-4301

333 W. Fourth St.
Room 3104
Tulsa, OK 74103
918/581-7495

Oregon
1220 S.W. Third Ave.
Room 676
Federal Building
Portland, OR 97204
503/221-5209

Pennsylvania
*One Bala Cynwyd Plaza
231 St. Asaphs Rd
Suite 640
West Lobby
Bala Cynwyd, PA 19004
215/596-5889

One Bala Cynwyd Plaza
231 St. Asaphs Rd.
Suite 400
East Lobby
Bala Cynwyd, PA 19004

Regional Office

100 Chestnut St.
Room 309
Harrisburg, PA 17101
717/782-3840

1000 Liberty Ave.
Room 1401
Pittsburgh, PA 15222
412/644-2780

Penn Place
20 N. Pennsylvania Ave.
Wilkes-Barre, PA 18702
717/826-6497

Puerto Rico
Federal Building
Room 6991
Carlos Chardon Ave.
Hato Rey, PR 00919
809/753-4572

Rhode Island
40 Fountain St.
Providence, RI 02903
401/528-4586

South Carolina
1835 Assembly St.
3rd Floor
PO Box 2786
Columbia, SC 29201
803/765-5376

South Dakota
101 South Main Ave.
Suite 101
Sioux Falls, SD 57102
605/336-2980

Tennessee
Fidelity Bankers Bldg.
502 South Gay St.
Room 307
Knoxville, TN 37902
615/251-5881

211 Federal Office Bldg.
167 North Main St.
Memphis, TN 38103
901/521-3588

404 James Robertson Pkwy.
Suite 1012

Nashville, TN 37219
615/251-5881

Texas
Federal Building
Room 780
300 East 8th St.
Austin, TX 78701
512/397-5288

3105 Leopard St.
PO Box 9253
Corpus Christi, TX 78408
512/888-3331

*1720 Regal Row
Room 230
Dallas, TX 75235
214/767-7643

1100 Commerce St.
Room 3C36
Dallas, TX 75242
214/767-0605

4100 Rio Bravo St.
Suite 300
Pershing W. Bldg.
El Paso, TX 79902
915/534-7586

222 E. Van Buren St.
Suite 500
Harlingen, TX 78550
512/423-4533

2525 Murthworth
#705
Houston, TX 77054
713/660-2409

1205 Texas Ave.
Room 712
Lubbock, TX 79401
806/762-7466

100 South Washington St.
Room G-12
Marshall, TX 75670
214/935-5257

727 E. Durango St.

Room A-513
Federal Bldg.
San Antonio, TX 78206
512/229-6260

Utah
125 South State Street
Room 2237
Salt Lake City, UT 84138
801/524-5800

Vermont
87 State St
Room 204
Montpelier, VT 05602
802/229-0538

Virginia
400 North 18th St
Room 3015
PO Box 10126
Richmond, VA 23240
804/771-2617

Virgin Islands
Veterans Drive
Room 283
St Thomas, VI 00801
809/774-8530

Washington
*710 2nd Ave.
5th Floor
Seattle, WA 98104
206/442-5676

915 Second Ave.
Room 1744
Seattle, WA 98174
206/442-5534

651 U.S. Courthouse
PO Box 2167
Spokane, WA 99210
509/456-5310

West Virginia
109 North 3rd St.
Room 301
Clarksburg, WV 26301
304/623-5631

Charleston National Plaza
Suite 628

Regional Office

Charleston, WV 25301
304/343-6181

Wisconsin
500 South Barstow St.
Room 89AA
Eau Claire, WI 54701
715/834-9012

212 E. Washington Ave.
Room 213
Madison, WI 53703

608/264-5205

517 E. Wisconsin Ave.
Room 246
Milwaukee, WI 53202
414/291-3941

Wyoming
PO Box 2839
Casper, WY 82602
307/265-5550

SBA Publications

These are free publications currently available from the SBA. The Management Aids (MAs) recommend methods and techniques for handling management problems and business operations. Small Business Bibliographies (SBBs) list key reference sources for many business management topics. Starting Out Series (SOSs) are one-page fact sheets describing financial and operating requirements for selected manufacturing, retail, and service businesses. They may be ordered from: U.S. Small Business Administration, Box 15434, Ft. Worth, TX 76119.

Management Aids

Financial Management and Analysis

MA 1.001	*The ABC's of Borrowing*
MA 1.002	*What Is the Best Selling Price?*
MA 1.003	*Keep Pointed toward Profit*
MA 1.004	*Basic Budgets for Profit Planning*
MA 1.005	*Pricing for Small Manufacturers*
MA 1.006	*Cash Flow in a Small Plant*
MA 1.007	*Credit and Collections*
MA 1.008	*Attacking Business Decision Problems with Breakeven Analysis*
MA 1.009	*A Venture Capital Primer for Small Business*
MA 1.010	*Accounting Services for Small Service Firms*
MA 1.011	*Analyze Your Records to Reduce Costs*

MA 1.012   *Profit by Your Wholesalers' Services*
MA 1.013   *Steps in Meeting Your Tax Obligations*
MA 1.014   *Getting the Facts for Income Tax Reporting*
MA 1.015   *Budgeting in a Small Business Firm*
MA 1.016   *Sound Cash Management and Borrowing*
MA 1.017   *Keeping Records in Small Business*
MA 1.018   *Check List for Profit Watching*
MA 1.019   *Simple Breakeven Analysis for Small Stores*
MA 1.020   *Profit Pricing and Costing for Services*

Planning

MA 2.002   *Locating or Relocating Your Business*
MA 2.004   *Problems in Managing a Family-Owned Business*
MA 2.005   *The Equipment Replacement Decision*
MA 2.006   *Finding a New Product for Your Company*
MA 2.007   *Business Plan for Small Manufacturers*
MA 2.008   *Business Plan for Small Construction Firms*
MA 2.009   *Business Life Insurance*
MA 2.010   *Planning and Goal Setting for Small Business*
MA 2.011   *Fixing Production Mistakes*
MA 2.012   *Setting up a Quality Control System*
MA 2.013   *Can You Make Money with Your Idea or Invention?*
MA 2.014   *Can You Lease or Buy Equipment?*
MA 2.015   *Can You Use a Minicomputer?*
MA 2.016   *Check List for Going into Business*
MA 2.017   *Factors in Considering a Shopping Center*
MA 2.018   *Insurance Checklist for Small Business*
MA 2.019   *Computers for Small Business—Service Bureau or Time Sharing*
MA 2.020   *Business Plan for Retailers*
MA 2.021   *Using a Traffic Study to Select a Retail Site*
MA 2.022   *Business Plan for Small Service Firms*
MA 2.024   *Store Location: "Little Things" Mean a Lot*
MA 2.025   *Thinking About Going into Business?*

General Management and Administration

Marketing

Organization and Personnel

Legal and Governmental Affairs

MA 6.003   *Incorporating a Small Business*
MA 6.004   *Selecting the Legal Structure for Your Business*
MA 6.005   *Introduction to Patents*

Miscellaneous

MA 7.002   *Association Services for Small Business*
MA 237   *Market Overseas with U.S. Government Help*

Small Business Bibliographies

1. *Handcrafts*
2. *Home Business*
3. *Selling by Mail Order*
9. *Marketing Research Procedures*
10. *Retailing*
12. *Statistics and Maps for National Market Analysis*
13. *National Directory for Use in Marketing*
15. *Recordkeeping Systems—Small Store and Service Trade*
18. *Basic Library Reference Sources*
20. *Advertising—Retail Store*
31. *Retail Credit and Collection*
37. *Buying for Retail Stores*
72. *Personnel Management*
75. *Inventory Management*
85. *Purchasing for Owners of Small Plants*
86. *Training for Small Business*
87. *Financial Management*
88. *Manufacturing Management*
89. *Marketing for Small Business*
90. *New Product Development*
91. *Ideas into Dollars*

Starting Out Series

0101   *Building Service Contracting*
0104   *Radio-Television Repair Shop*

0105   *Retail Florists*

0106   *Franchised Businesses*

0107   *Hardware Store or Home Centers*

0111   *Sporting Goods Store*

0112   *Drycleaning*

0114   *Cosmetology*

0115   *Pest Control*

0116   *Marine Retailers*

0117   *Retail Grocery Stores*

0122   *Apparel Store*

0123   *Pharmacies*

0125   *Office Products*

0129   *Interior Design Services*

0130   *Fish Farming*

0133   *Bicycles*

0134   *Roofing Contractors*

0135   *Printing*

0137   *The Bookstore*

0138   *Home Furnishings*

0142   *Ice Cream*

0145   *Sewing Centers*

0148   *Personnel Referral Service*

0149   *Selling by Mail Order*

0150   *Solar Energy*

0201   *Breakeven Point for Independent Truckers*

Order from:
  U.S. Small Business Administration
  Box 15434
  Ft Worth, TX 76119

Resource Literature

Basic Research

Daniells, Lorna M.: *Business Information Sources,* rev. ed., University of California Press, Los Angeles, 1985.

Way, James (ed.): *Encyclopedia of Business Information Sources,* 6th ed., Gale Research, Detroit, 1986.

Brownstone, David M., and Gorton Carruth: *Where to Find Business Information: A Worldwide Guide for Everyone Who Needs Answers to Business Questions,* Wiley-Interscience, New York, 1982.

Schlessigner, Bernard S., (ed.): *The Basic Business Library: Core Resources,* Oryx Press, Phoenix, 1983.

Johnson, Webster H., Anthony J. Faria, and Ernest L. Maier: *How to Use the Business Library with Sources of Information,* 5th ed., South-Western Publishing Co., Cincinnati, 1984.

Small Business Sourcebook, Gale Research Co., Detroit, 1984. This is a very comprehensive source.

Part 1 profiles 100 common small businesses and provides information about:

- Associations
- Educational programs
- Reference works
- Sources of supply
- Trade periodicals
- Trade shows
- Conventions
- Consultants
- Franchises
- Other sources of information

Part 2 compiles information resources for small businesses in general. It organizes the nearly 1000 sources of information by sector:

- Federal government
- State and local government
- Trade and professional associations
- Educational institutions
- Consultants

· Venture capital firms
· Published sources of information

To Help You Search for the Business

U.S. Business Directories: 600 Directories Compiled From Yellow Pages, American Business Directors, Omaha, annual.
Lists of 14 Million Businesses Compiled From the Yellow Pages, American Business Lists, Omaha, annual.
The National Business List, Market Data Retrieval, Shelton, CT, quarterly.
Colgate, Craig, Jr., (ed.): *National Trade and Professional Associations of the United States,* 18th ed., Columbia Books, New York, 1983.
Ross, Marilyn, (ed.): *Career Women's Network Directory: An Up-to-Date, Complete Listing of Professional Organizations and Contacts,* Communications Creativity, Saquacher, CO, 1986.
Etheridge, James M., (ed.): *The Directory of Directories,* Gale Research Co., Detroit, 1985.
Gruber, Katherine, (ed.): *Encyclopedia of Associations,* 20th ed., Gale Research Co., Detroit, 1986.
Direct Mail List Rates and Data, Standard Rate and Data Service, Skokie, IL.
Polk Mailing List Catalog, R.L. Polk & Co., Taylor, MI.
Catalog of Mailing Lists, F.S. Hoffheimer, Mineola, NY.
Duns Marketing Services, Parsippany, NJ.
Thomas Register of American Manufacturers and Thomas Register Catalog File, Thomas Publishing Co., New York, annual.

Analyzing the Business

Kohl, John C., Sr., and Atlee M. Kohl: *The Smart Way to Buy a Business: An Entrepreneur's Guide to Questions That Must Be Asked,* Woodland Publishers, Irving, TX, 1986.
Tray, Leo: *Almanac of Business and Industrial Ratios,* Prentice-Hall, Englewood Cliffs, NJ, annual.
Bowlin, Oswald D.: *Guide to Financial Analysis,* McGraw-Hill, New York, 1979.
Sweeny, Allen: *Accounting Fundamentals for Non-Financial Executives,* Amacom, New York, 1972.
Pratt, Shannon: *Valuing a Business: The Analysis and Appraisal of Closely Held Companies,* Dow Jones-Irwin, Homewood, IL, 1983.
Pratt, Shannon, *Valuing Small Businesses and Professional Practices,* Dow Jones-Irwin, Homewood, IL, 1985.
Miles, Raymond C.: *Basic Business Appraisal,* John Wiley, New York, 1984.
Tracy, J. A.: *How to Read a Financial Report: Wringing Cash Flow and Other Vital Signs Out of the Numbers,* 2d ed., John Wiley, New York, 1985.
Hayes, Rick S., and C. Richard Baker: *Simplified Accounting for Non-Accountants,* John Wiley, New York, 1980.

Sources of Financing

Robins, Adam E.: *Getting Your Banker to Say "Yes": Tactics for the Entrepreneur,* Probus, New York, 1985.

Silver, A. David: *Up Front Financing: The Entrepreneurs Guide*, John Wiley, New York, 1982.

Pratt, Stanley E., and Jane K. Morris, (eds.): *Pratt's Guide to Venture Capital Sources*, 10th ed., Venture Economics, Inc., Oryx Press, Phoenix, 1986.

Silver, A. David: *Who's Who In Venture Capital*, 2nd ed., John Wiley, New York, 1986.

Small Business Financing, Shepard's-McGraw-Hill, New York, 1983.

Weissman, Rudolph L.: *Small Business and Venture Capital*, Ayer Co., Salem, NH, 1979.

Haft, Robert J.: *Venture Capital and Small Business Financing*, Boardman, 1984.

Hayes, Stephen R., and John C. Howell: *How to Finance Your Small Business with Government Money: SBA and Other Loans*, 2d ed., John Wiley, New York, 1983.

Holtz, Herman: *2001 Sources of Financing for Small Businesses*, Arco Publishing, New York, 1983.

Franchising

Small, Samuel, and Pilot Books Staff, *Directory of Franchising Organizations*, Pilot Books, New York, 1986.

Franchise Annual: Handbook and Directory, Info Press, Lewiston, NY, annual.

Franchise Opportunities Handbook, Office of Consumer Goods and Service Industries, U.S. Dept. of Commerce, U.S. Government Printing Office, Washington, D.C., 20402.

Negotiating and Closing

Raiffa, Howard: *The Art and Science of Negotiating*, The Belknap Press of Harvard University Press, Cambridge, MA, 1982.

Fisher, Roger, and William Ury: *Getting to Yes: Negotiating Agreement Without Giving In*, Houghton Mifflin, Boston, 1983.

Lane, Marc J.: *Legal Handbook for Small Business*, American Management Association, New York, 1978.

Rohrlich, Chester A.: *Organizing Corporate and Other Business Enterprises*, Matthew Bender & Co., New York, 1986.

Goldstein, Arnold: *Business Transfers*, John Wiley, New York, 1984.

Nierenberg, Gerard I.: *Creative Business Negotiating: Skills and Successful Strategies*, Hawthorn Books, New York, 1971.

General Reading

Mancuso, Joseph: *Have You Got What It Takes: How to Tell If You Should Start Your Own Business*, Prentice-Hall, Englewood Cliffs, NJ, 1982.

Rausch, E.: *Financial Management for Small Business*, Amacom, New York, 1982.

Williams, Edward E., and Salvatore E. Manzo: *Business Planning for the Entrepreneur*, Van Nostrand Reinhold, New York, 1983.

Mucciolo, Louis: *Small Business: Look Before You Leap. A Catalog of Sources of Information to Help You Start and Manage Your Own Small Business*, Arco Publishing, New York, 1981.

Cushman, Robert F.: *Business Insurance Handbook*, Dow Jones-Irwin, Inc., Homewood, IL, 1981.

Hancock, William A.: *The Small Business Legal Advisor*, McGraw-Hill, New York, 1982.

Smith, Brian R., and Thomas L. West: *Buying Your Own Small Business,* The Stephen Greene Press, Lexington, MA, 1985.

For the New Owner

Lasser (J. K.) Tax Institute: *How to Own A Small Business,* McGraw-Hill, New York, 1985.
Bumback, Clifford M.: *How to Organize and Operate a Small Business,* 7th ed., Prentice-Hall, Englewood Cliffs, NJ, 1985.
Curtin, Richard: *Running Your Own Show: Mastering the Basics of Small Business,* New American Library, New York, 1983.
Park, William R., and Sue Chapin-Park: *How to Succeed in Your Own Business,* John Wiley, New York, 1978.
Silvester, James L.: *How to Start, Finance, and Operate Your Own Business,* Lyle Stuart, Secaucus, NJ, 1984.
Lowry, Albert J.: *How to Become Financially Successful by Owning Your Own Business,* Simon & Schuster, New York, 1981.
The Small Business Reporter, Bank of America, Dept. 3120, San Francisco (a series of short books):

Guide to Tax Reform	Management Transitions
Business Computers from A to Z	Steps to Starting a Business
How to Buy and Sell a Business or Franchise	Business Financing
Marketing Small Business	Understanding Financial Statements
Cash Flow/Cash Management	Financial Records for Small Business
Avoiding Management Pitfalls	Personnel Guidelines
Crime Prevention for Small Business	Equipment Leasing
Establishing an Accounting Practice	Establishing a Dental Practice
Establishing a Medical Practice	

Newspapers and Magazines

Finders International, Hawley, PA, quarterly.
Business Opportunities Digest, Clarksville, TN, monthly.
Business Opportunities Journal, San Diego, monthly.
Business and Acquisition Newsletter, Newsletters International, Houston, monthly.
Mergers and Acquisitions, MLR Enterprises, Inc., Philadelphia, bi-monthly.
Entrepreneur Magazine, American Entrepreneur's Association, Los Angeles, monthly.
Inc., The Magazine for Growing Companies, Boston, monthly.
Success Magazine, New York, monthly.

Venture Magazine, New York, monthly.

Basic Computer Software

Word Processing

Multimate, Ashton-Tate.   Multimate Advantage, Ashton-Tate
Wordstar, Micro-Pro International.   Wordstar 2000, Micro-Pro International

Database (Files and Records) Management

dBase III Plus, Ashton-Tate.   Cornerstone, Infocom, Inc.
DataEase, Software Solutions.   Alpha/Three, Alpha Software Corporation

Financial Analysis and Planning

Javelin, Javelin Software Corporation.   Money Decision Financial Desk Reference, Silver Eagle Software Publishing

Spreadsheets

IBM Planning Assistant, IBM Corporation.   Lotus 1-2-3, Lotus Development Corporation
Microsoft Multiplan, Microsoft Corporation.   SuperCalc 4, Computer Associates

Appendix F
Company Profile Data Form

Company Profile Data Form

1. General Information

Source of contact

Co. name _____   _____

Address _____   _____

_____   _____

_____   Date _____

Owner's name _____

Phone _____   _____
        Business   Home

Business description _____

_____

_____

How owned: sole proprietor _____ partnership _____ corporation _____ type of corp. _____

Reason for selling: _____

Seller will not compete for _____ years and _____ miles.

Seller will train: yes _____ no _____ . how long: _____ .

What are the outstanding features of the business? _____

_____

Special skills or licenses needed: _____

Business hours: _____

Current market conditions and outlook: _____

2. Price and Terms

Asking price: **$** _____ . Inventory included: **$** _____ . Additional: **$** _____ .

Type of sale: Asset _____ Stock _____ .

Seller desires _____ % of the total selling price as a down payment.

Seller will carry the balance at _____ % interest for _____ years.

Interest only: yes _____ no _____ . Balloon payment: yes _____ no _____ . After _____ years.

Any equipment leases to be assumed by the buyer? yes _____ no _____ .

Approximate total lease payments: **$** _____ per month for _____ years.

Seller will consider exchange: yes _____ no _____ . For _____ .
                                        (type of property)

Approximate inventory value at cost _____ as of _____ 19 _____ .

3. People

Owner's duties: _____

Key people

Title	Years Employed and Duties
_____	_____
_____	_____
_____	_____

Total employees excluding seller: _____ full time; _____ part time.

Overall assesment of people: _____

Owner's and key employee's status after sale _____

_____

Company Profile Data Form continued

4. Equipment, Furniture, Fixtures

Item	Age	Cost If Known	Estimated Value

5. Real Estate

Approx. size of lot: _____ sq ft/acres; property zoned: _____
Approx. number of parking spaces: _____
Number of buildings: _____ . Approx. size of building: _____ sq ft.
Type of construction (if known): _____
Approx. age of building: _____ ; Living quarters: yes _____ no _____
Storage area: yes _____ no _____ .Loading area: yes _____ no _____ . Repairs needed: yes _____ no _____
Is the real estate for sale? yes _____ no _____ Price: $ _____
Is the property for lease? yes _____ no _____ . Monthly rent: $ _____
Additional/override rent (if any): _____
Common area charge (if any): $ _____ . Original length of lease: _____
Time left on current lease: _____ . Expires (month and year): _____
Lease deposit (if any): $ _____ . Lease/purchase option: yes _____ no _____
Other options: _____
Is lease assumable? yes _____ no _____

6. Summary of financials

Income Statement
For the period _____ to _____

Sales		$ _____
Cost of sales	$ _____	
Gross profit		$ _____
Expenses		
Owner's salary		$ _____
Owner's benefits		_____
Employee salaries (no. of people _____)		_____
Employee benefits		_____
Rent		_____
Utilities		_____
Travel and entertainment		_____
Selling expenses		_____
Depreciation		_____
Insurance		_____
Interest		_____
Automobile		_____
Legal and accounting		_____
Other _____		_____
Other _____		_____
Other _____		_____
Total expenses		$ _____
Pretax profit		$ _____

Company Data Form continued

7. Evaluation

Rating verses criteria (Chapter 3)
Use 1 to 10 scale; 10 is best.

Cash flow	_____	Growth potential	_____
Location	_____	Working condition	_____
Liquidity	_____	Status and image	_____
People intensity	_____	Competition	_____
Overall desirability	_____	Content of the business	_____

Total _____ ÷ 10 = _____ rating

Risk evaluation (Chapter 4)
Use 1 to 6 scale: 6 is low risk.

Company history	_____	Special skills required	_____
The industry segment	_____	Special relationships required	_____
Location	_____	Labor situation	_____
Return *of* investment	_____	Management situation	_____
Return *on* investment	_____	Outside dependency	_____
Company reputation	_____	Products/services	_____
Competition	_____	Franchises/licenses required	_____
Technology	_____	Legal exposure	_____

Total _____ ÷ 16 = _____ rating

Company Data Form continued
Balance Sheet
as of _____

Current assets:
Cash $ _____
Accounts receivable   _____
Notes receivable   _____
Inventory   _____
Prepaid expenses   _____
Other   _____
Total Current Assets $ _____

Fixed assets:

Furniture, fixtures, machinery, and equipment $ _____
Less: accumulated depreciation   _____ $ _____
Land and buildings   _____
Less: accumulated depreciation   _____ $ _____
Other assets _____ $ _____
Total fixed assets $ _____
Total assets $ _____

Liabilities and Owner's Equity

Current liabilities:
Accounts payable $ _____
Wages payable   _____
Taxes payable   _____
Interest payable   _____
Notes/leases (current portion)   _____
Services or products owed to customers   _____
Other liabilities   _____
    Total current liabilities $ _____

Long-term liabilities:

Notes $ _____
Mortgages   _____
Other _____   _____
    Total long-term liabilities $ _____

Owner's equity:
Capital stock $ _____
Retained earnings   _____
    Total liabilities and owner's equity $ _____

Company Data Form continued

Contact Follow-Up Record

Date of Contact	With (Name)	Topics Discussed	Date to Follow Up

Index

ABOUT THE AUTHOR

C. D. "Pete" Peterson held executive positions at multinational companies such as International Paper and Merrill Lynch until he left the corporate world in 1984. He now runs his own business brokerage business, where he has worked with more than 2000 business seekers, whose firsthand experience provided the basis for this book. He holds a master's degree in management from MIT, where he was an Alfred P. Sloan Fellow.